PRINC

GW00368097

PRINCE2™ Revealed

Second edition

Colin Bentley

AMSTERDAM • BOSTON • HEIDELBERG • LONDON • NEW YORK • OXFORD
PARIS • SAN DIEGO • SAN FRANCISCO • SINGAPORE • SYDNEY • TOKYO

Butterworth-Heinemann is an imprint of Elsevier

Butterworth-Heinemann is an imprint of Elsevier
Linacre House, Jordan Hill, Oxford OX2 8DP, UK
30 Corporate Drive, Suite 400, Burlington, MA 01803, USA

First Edition 2006
Second Edition 2010

British Library Cataloguing in Publication Data
A catalogue record for this book is available from the British Library

Library of Congress Cataloging-in-Publication Data
A catalog record for this book is available from the Library of Congress

ISBN: 978-1-85617-813-6

For information on all Butterworth-Heinemann
publications visit our website at books.elsevier.com

Printed and bound in Great Britain

10 11   10 9 8 7 6 5 4 3 2

Contents

THE METHOD

This book presents the 2009 revision of PRINCE2, a structured project management method based on the experience of scores of project managers who have contributed to its development, some from their mistakes or omissions, others from their success. It can be applied to any kind of project, however big or small; the basic philosophy is always the same. The method should be tailored to suit the size, importance and environment of the project.

Those who are starting a project for the first time should not have to reinvent the wheel. They should be able to build on the experiences of previous project managers and these experiences show us why a good project management method such as PRINCE2 is needed if our projects are to be well managed and controlled.

Chapter 1

Introduction

PRINCE2™ is a Trade Mark of the Office of Government Commerce (OGC).

This book is based on the PRINCE2 project management method. This method is owned by the OGC, an agency of the British government, and has been put into the public domain by them, so there is no fee to be paid for its use. (If you want to make money from the method, e.g. by offering training, products or consultancy, you need to get approval from OGC or the APM Group, contactable through enquiries@apmg-uk.com).

This book is an overview of PRINCE2 for those readers who want an introduction to the method. It covers the whole method and aims to provide an understandable, end-to-end overview of the basics rather than a detailed exploration of the complexitites of PRINCE2.

1.1 WHAT IS A PROJECT?

Here are a few definitions of a project from Wikipedia. Each one adds something unique to a common thread.

"A project is a management environment created for the purpose of delivering one or more business products according to a specified business case."

"A project is a temporary structure created to achieve a specified business benefit or objective. When the work has been completed, the project team is disbanded."

"A project is a finite endeavor (having specific start and completion dates) undertaken to create a unique product or service which brings about beneficial change or added value."

Project management is the discipline of planning, organizing and managing resources to bring about the successful completion of specific project goals and objectives.

1.2 BENEFITS OF THE PRINCE2 PROJECT MANAGEMENT METHOD

Organizations are becoming increasingly aware of the opportunities for adopting a 'project' approach to the way in which they address the creation and delivery of new business products or implement any change. They are also increasingly aware of the benefits which a single, common, structured approach to project management – as is provided through PRINCE2 – can bring.

PRINCE2 is a scalable, flexible project management method, derived from the experience of professional project managers and refined over years of use in a wide variety of contexts. It is owned by a stable public authority, OGC is part of the Treasury. The OGC has an ongoing commitment to maintaining the currency of the method and the tools which go with it, together with the information, books and manuals used to define the method.

- The method is repeatable.
- It is teachable.
- It builds on experience.
- It can be applied to any type or size of project.
- It insists that there should be a viable business case for a project before it begins and continues.
- It focuses on quality throughout the project life cycle.
- It clearly identifies project responsibilities.
- Everyone knows what to expect.
- It defines a thorough but economical structure of reports.

- It is based on management by exception, which gives efficient and effective use of management time.
- It ensures good communications with all stakeholders throughout the project.
- There is early warning of problems.
- If you take over a project in the middle, you know what documents to look for and where to find them.
- It is proactive not reactive (but has to be prepared to be reactive to events – illness, pregnancy, accident, external events).

1.3 FINANCE

Use of this method is free. There is no purchase price and no annual licence fee for users.

1.4 SUPPORT

- The owner of the method, the OGC, has made a commitment to support its continuing evolution.
- The method was and is developed and enhanced by practising, professional project managers.
- There is a strong user group (in the UK, The Netherlands, Germany and Australia at present).
- PRINCE2 can be used for all types and sizes of projects, encouraging its spread throughout organizations.
- The method is supported by over 20 specialist books.
- There is increasing software tool support for the method.
- There are regular examinations for project managers and also for project support personnel and those on the periphery of projects, such as auditors and quality assurance personnel.
- The foundation and practitioner exam certificates, issued on behalf of OGC, are recognized world-wide.
- Over 1 million candidates have taken the practitioner exam in the UK so far. There are thousands more who have taken the exams in The Netherlands, Australia and the U.S.A.

- A number of UK companies have included PRINCE2 certification in their project management career path.
- Many UK project management advertisements in the national press ask for PRINCE2 knowledge or certification.

1.5 INTERNATIONAL SPREAD

- The method and exams are recognized and used in many countries, including the UK, The Netherlands, Denmark, Scandinavia, Poland, Hungary, Switzerland, Australia, North and South America, South Africa, China, Hong Kong, Singapore, Italy, Bulgaria and Indonesia.
- The method has public and private sector users.
- Books on the method are available in many other languages, such as Dutch, German, French, Italian, Polish, Danish, Chinese and Spanish.

1.6 QUALITY CONTROL

- In order for any firm to be able to offer training or consultancy in the method to other organizations, the APM Group has to first formally accredit it. This accreditation has the following three parts:
  1. The company has to show that it has the procedures and administrative capacity to provide and support courses.
  2. The training material and course timetable are checked against the method and the syllabus.
  3. Each trainer in the method must have passed both foundation and practitioner examinations, and scored well in the practitioner examination. The trainer must have a CV that shows solid project management experience. Each trainer is observed by the APM Group representative actually giving one or more sessions, and is then quizzed on their understanding of the method in general.
- All course delegates are asked to complete a feedback form, which is sent to the APM Group. A check is kept for any quality

problems that may be voiced. If any arise, these are taken up with the management of the training organization.

- Every trainer is subject to continuous accreditation. Where a trainer cannot provide evidence of regular presentation experience in the method, he or she may be asked to go through the initial accreditation process again.
- Exam setting and marking is done by the APM Group, completely independently of the training organizations.
- Representatives of the APM Group may make ad-hoc visits to any PRINCE2 course.
- When the manual has been revised, each training organization's material is reviewed. Training organizations are given advanced warning of the manual changes to allow them to time the introduction of the new material with the publication of the revised manual.

1.7 PUBLICITY

The APM Group has two well-established Web sites, http://www.prince2.org.uk and http://www.apmgroup.co.uk.

- These contain details of all accredited training organizations and consultants, as well as a bookshop and a list of all those who have passed the exams. A future Web site will carry in-depth articles on the method to encourage regular visits by users.
- Magazine articles are regularly written for UK project management magazines.

Chapter 2

An Overview of PRINCE2

2.1 PROJECT CHARACTERISTICS

The finite characteristic of projects stands in contrast to processes, or operations, which are permanent or semi-permanent functional work to repetitively produce the same product or service (Business as Usual or BAU for short). In practice, the management of these two types of work is often found to be quite different, and as such requires the development of distinct technical skills and the adoption of separate management.

There are at least five characteristics of project work that separate it from BAU:

- **Change:** We use projects to introduce change to a business.
- **Uncertainty:** A project changes one or more things or develops something new. These are steps into the unknown, introducing uncertainty in what will be ahead of us in the project.
- **Temporary:** A team comes together for a project, does a job and is then disbanded.
- **Unique:** In some major or minor ways each project is unique. It may be completely unlike anything we have done before, or we may have repeated the same job several times, but at a different location or with different people.
- **Cross-functional:** A project needs different people with different skills; some to define what is required, others to develop the required products. Another problem is that they probably work

for several different line managers, maybe even different companies. So managing these resources is another problem for the Project Manager.

2.2 PROJECT PERFORMANCE ASPECTS

There are six aspects of project performance that always need to be managed:

- **Costs:** Always a problem; estimating how much it will cost, then controlling efficiency and effectiveness to ensure that this cost is not exceeded.
- **Timescales:** How long will the project take? How effective will resources be? Have you made allowances for meetings, training, learning cycles?
- **Quality:** More important than getting cost and time right is getting the quality right. Do you know what quality the customer wants? Have you allowed enough time and resources to achieve that quality?
- **Scope:** How precisely are the requirements known? Have you got an agreed cut-off of finalizing requirements? Have you got a change control procedure in place to avoid 'scope creep'? Does the customer understand that any changes to the specification after you have agreed on a price and timeframe must be paid for?
- **Risk:** Have we reviewed the project for risks at the outset? Are we regularly reviewing risks? Have we a risk management procedure in place? Do we know what level of risk the customer is willing to take?
- **Benefits:** Are there valid reasons for doing the project? Does the outcome fit with company strategy? Are the claimed benefits realistic? Do we have measurements of the situation before the outcome is delivered in order to measure the achievement of benefits?

PRINCE2 contains the processes and themes that will keep these aspects under control.

2.3 PRINCIPLES OF PRINCE2

There are seven principles on which PRINCE2 is founded (Figure 2.1). This set of principles is unique to the PRINCE2 method.

The principles are characterized as:

- Universal: They apply to every project.
- Self-validating: They have been proved by use over many years.
- Empowering: They give users of the method the ability to shape the management of the project.

The seven PRINCE2 principles are:

- Continued business justification;
- Learn from experience;
- Defined roles and responsibilities;
- Manage by stages;
- Manage by exception;
- Focus on products;
- Tailored to suit the project environment.

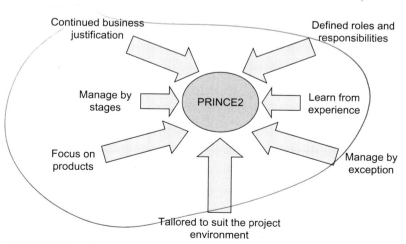

FIGURE 2.1   The seven PRINCE2 Principles.

2.3.1 Continued Business Justification

(A project should be driven by its Business Case)

PRINCE2 emphasizes that a viable Business Case should drive a project. Its existence should be proved before the project is given the go-ahead and it should be confirmed at all major decision points during the project. It should also be documented. (If a product fails to deliver all the expected benefits, those who originally claimed that the benefits would be there may suffer from amnesia.)

So,

- You should not start a project unless there is a sound Business Case for it.
- At regular intervals in the project you should check to see that the project is still viable.
- Stop the project if the justification has disappeared.

The Business Case:
- Is documented and approved;
- Drives the decision-making processes;
- Ensures the project remains aligned to the business objectives and benefits being sought.

Even projects that are compulsory require justification – there may be several options available that yield different costs, benefits and risks.

Justification may change, but must remain valid.

2.3.2 Learn from Experience

Project management should never be 're-inventing the wheel'. Those involved in the project may have previous experience; there will be earlier projects in the company from which lessons can be learned and there are other sources (e.g. the web, suppliers, sister companies) of valuable lessons that can be used in the project.

Lessons should be sought at the beginning of a project (in the process *Starting up a Project*), learned as the project progresses and passed on to other projects after the close.

2.3.3 Defined Roles and Responsibilities

Project management is different from line management.

Projects require a temporary organization for a finite timescale for a specific business purpose. Managing the project staff can be a headache for a Project Manager. A project is temporary and may include staff who report to different line managers or even work for other organizations. A project may require a mixture of full-time and part-time resources. So how do we have everyone know who is responsible for what?

An explicit project management team structure is required. People must know what their and other people's responsibilities are. Good communication depends on this.

The roles and responsibilities are divided into three groups, the interests of which must be represented in any project (Figure 2.2). These are:

- Business;
- User;
- Supplier.

PRINCE2 provides an organization structure that engages everyone involved: the business, user and supplier stakeholder interests.

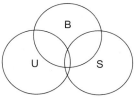

FIGURE 2.2   Business, user and supplier interests.

Within the structure there are defined roles and responsibilities for every member of the project management team. The chosen people agree to a role description and sign their acceptance of that role. (Depending on the size of the project, roles can be split or combined.)

2.3.4 Manage by Stages

This comes from two different thoughts:

1. If the Project Board is, in PRINCE2 terms, ultimately accountable for the project and PRINCE2 does not like the idea of regular progress meetings, there must be some key points in a project when the Project Board needs to review progress and decide if it wants to continue with the project.
2. Very often a project will last longer and contain more detail than can be planned with any accuracy at the outset.

Based on these thoughts, PRINCE2 divides a project into stages. PRINCE2 has a Project Plan, an overview of the whole project, which is often a 'best guess', but the Project Manager plans only the next stage in detail – only as much as can be accurately judged – and the Project Board approves only one stage at a time, reviewing the status at stage end and deciding whether to continue or not.

The number of stages depends on the size, complexity and risk content of the project.

At the end of each stage, a plan is presented, together with an updated view of the Business Case, the Project Plan, the risks and suggested tolerances for the next stage. Thus senior management can review progress so far and decide from the information presented to them whether or not to authorize the next stage.

2.3.5 Manage by Exception

PRINCE2 recognizes four levels of authority in a project. Authority is delegated from one management level to the next. Each management level is allocated tolerances within which it can continue without the need to refer to the next higher level of management. There are six tolerance limits:

1. Time: +/− an amount of time on the target completion dates.
2. Cost: +/− amounts of planned budget.
3. Quality: +/− degrees off a quality target, e.g. a product that weighs a target 10 k (with an allowed −50 g to +10 g tolerance).
4. Scope: Permissible variation of the plan's products, e.g. mandatory requirements +/− desirable requirements.
5. Risk: Limits on the plan's exposure to threats (e.g. the risk of not meeting the target date against the risk of overspending).
6. Benefit: +/− degrees off an improvement goal (e.g. 30% to 40% staff saving).

To cut down on unnecessary meetings or problem referrals, PRINCE2 has the principle of allowing a management level to continue its work as long as there is no forecast that a tolerance will be exceeded. Only when there is a forecast of a tolerance being exceeded does the next higher level of authority need to be consulted.

2.3.6 Focus on Products

A PRINCE2 project focuses on the definition and delivery of products, in particular their quality requirements. Planning, controls and quality needs are all product-based.

2.3.7 Tailor to Suit the Project Environment

PRINCE2 is tailored to suit the project's environment, size, risk, complexity, importance and capability of the people involved. Tailoring is considered before the project begins; roles may be split or combined, processes and documents may be combined, it may be agreed that some reports can be oral and some decisions made by phone or email rather than at meetings.

2.4 STRUCTURE OF THE PRINCE2 METHOD

There are three parts to the structure of the method itself:

- Processes;
- Key themes;
- Techniques.

The method offers a set of *processes* that provide a controlled start, a controlled progress and a controlled close to any project. The processes explain what should happen and when it should happen.

The method has a number of *themes* to explain its philosophy about various project aspects, why they are needed and how they can be used. This philosophy is implemented through the processes.

The method offers only a few *techniques*. The use of most of them is optional. You may already have a technique which is covering that need satisfactorily. The exception is the product-based planning technique. This is a very important part of PRINCE2. Its understanding and use bring major benefits and every effort should be made to use it.

2.5 THEMES

Figure 2.3 shows the themes positioned around the central process model.

The themes of PRINCE2 are:

Business Case	PRINCE2 emphasizes that a viable Business Case should drive a project. Its existence should be proved before the project is given a go-ahead and it should be confirmed at all major decision points during the project. Claimed benefits should be defined in measurable terms, so that they can be checked after delivery of the product.

Organization	The structure of a project management team. A definition of the roles, responsibilities and relationships of all staff involved in the project. PRINCE2 describes the roles. According to the size and complexity of a project, these roles can be combined or shared.
Plans	PRINCE2 offers a series of plan levels that can be tailored to the size and needs of a project, and an approach to planning based on products rather than activities.
Progress	A set of controls that facilitate the provision of key decision-making information, allowing the organization to preempt problems and make decisions for problem resolution. For senior management, PRINCE2 controls are based on the concept of 'management by exception', i.e. if we agree on a plan, let the manager get on with it unless something is forecasted to go wrong.
	A project is split into stages as an approach to defining the review and commitment points of a project in order to promote sound management control of risk and investment.
Risk	Risk is a major factor to be considered during the life of a project. PRINCE2 defines the key moments when risks should be reviewed, outlines an approach to the analysis and management of risk and tracks these through all the processes.
Quality	PRINCE2 recognizes the importance of quality and incorporates a quality approach to the management and technical processes. It begins by establishing the customer's quality expectations and follows these up by laying down standards and quality inspection methods to be used, and checking that these are being used.
Change	This contains two complementary activities: managing changes and managing the products.
	PRINCE2 emphasizes the need for change control and this is enforced with a change control technique plus identification of the themes that apply the change control.
	Tracking the components of a final product and their versions for release is called configuration management. There are many methods of configuration management available. PRINCE2 does not attempt to invent a new one, but defines the essential facilities and information requirements for a configuration management method and how it should link with other PRINCE2 themes and techniques.

FIGURE 2.3   PRINCE2 themes.

2.6 THE PROCESSES

The steps of project management are described in seven processes, which are summarized in Figure 2.4. The processes describe the chronological flow through a project.

Any project run under PRINCE2 will need to address each of these processes in some form. However, the key to successful use of the process model is in tailoring it to the needs of the individual project. Each process should be approached with the question 'How extensively should this process be applied on this project?'

A typical flow through the processes in a project is shown in Figure 2.5.

The 'Directing a Project' process has been split into its five parts to show the points at which they are used.

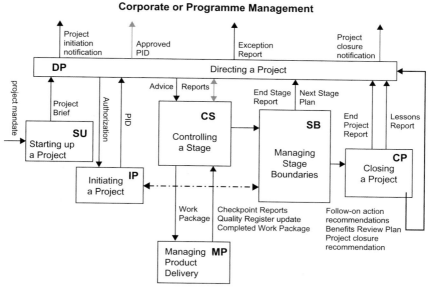

FIGURE 2.4   PRINCE2 processes.

2.6.1 Directing a Project (DP)

This process is aimed at the senior management team responsible for the project, the key decision-makers. These are usually very busy people and should be involved in only the decision-making process of a project. PRINCE2 helps them achieve this by adopting the principle of 'management by exception'. The DP process covers the activities by this senior management team (the Project Board) throughout the project from start-up to project closure and has five major steps:

- Authorizing the preparation of a Project Plan and Business Case for the project;
- Approving the project go-ahead;
- Checking that the project remains justifiable at key points in the project life cycle;
- Monitoring progress and giving advice as required;
- Ensuring that the project comes to a controlled close.

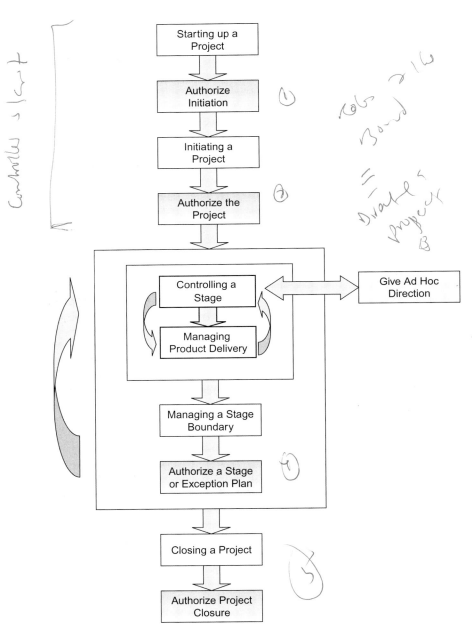

FIGURE 2.5 A typical flow through the PRINCE2 processes.

2.6.2 Starting Up a Project (SU)

This is intended to be a very short pre-project process with six objectives:

- Ensure that the scope of the project is known.
- Ensure there is business justification for initiating the project.
- Design and appoint the project management team.
- Decide on the approach which will be taken within the project to do the work.
- Agree upon the customer's quality expectations.
- Plan the work needed to draw up the PRINCE2 'contract' between the customer and the supplier.

2.6.3 Initiating a Project (IP)

This process prepares the information on whether there is sufficient justification to proceed with the project, establishes a sound management basis for the project and creates a detailed plan for as much of the project as management are in a position to authorize. The management product created is the Project Initiation Documentation, the baseline against which project progress and success will be measured.

2.6.4 Controlling a Stage (CS)

This process describes the monitoring and control activities of the Project Manager involved in ensuring that a stage stays on course and reacts to unexpected events. The process forms the core of the Project Manager's effort on the project, being the process that handles day-to-day management of the project development activity.

Throughout a stage there will be many cycles of:

- Authorizing work to be done;
- Gathering progress information about that work;
- Monitoring and controlling changes;
- Reviewing the situation;

- Reporting;
- Taking any necessary corrective action.

The process covers these activities, together with the ongoing work of risk management and change control.

2.6.5 Managing Product Delivery (MP)

The process covers:

- Making sure that work allocated to the team is authorized and agreed upon;
- Planning the team work;
- Ensuring that the work is done;
- Ensuring that products meet the agreed quality criteria;
- Obtaining acceptance of the finished products;
- Reporting on progress and quality to the Project Manager.

The process acts as a control mechanism so that the Project Manager and specialist teams can agree on the details of the work required. This is particularly important when one or more teams are from third-party suppliers not using PRINCE2. The work agreed upon between the Project Manager and the Team Manager, including target dates, quality and reporting requirements, is called a Work Package.

2.6.6 Managing a Stage Boundary (SB)

The objectives of this process are to:

- Plan the next stage;
- Assure the Project Board that all products of the current stage have been completed and accepted;
- Update the Project Plan;
- Update the Business Case;
- Update the risk assessment;
- Report on the outcome and performance of the stage which has just ended;

- Obtain Project Board approval to move into the next stage.

If the Project Board requests the Project Manager to produce an Exception Plan (see 'Controls' for an explanation), this process also covers the steps needed for that.

2.6.7 Closing a Project (CP)

The process covers the Project Manager's work to request Project Board permission to close the project either at its natural end or at a premature close decided by the Project Board. The objectives are to:

- Note the extent to which the objectives set out at the start of the project have been met;
- Confirm the customer's satisfaction with the products;
- Confirm that maintenance and support arrangements are in place (where appropriate);
- Make any recommendations for follow-on actions;
- Ensure that all lessons gathered during the project are annotated for the benefit of future projects;
- Report on whether the project management activity itself has been a success or not;
- Prepare a plan to check on achievement of the final product's claimed benefits.

Having gone through an introduction and overview of the method, the section will now focus on the processes as the main link. This will provide a project skeleton, a general project timeframe. Where appropriate there will be links to the themes and techniques, descriptions of which follow the processes.

Chapter 3

Starting Up a Project (SU)

A PRINCE2 project is triggered by a project mandate, a request to provide a solution to a business problem. Ideally it should have the information required to form the Project Brief, but as it is created before the project begins, there may be no control over its content. Part of the work of *Starting up a Project* is to fill in any gaps (Figure 3.1).

3.0.1 What Does the Process Do?

- Receives a project mandate;
- Confirms the existence of (or completes) adequate terms of reference for the project;
- Creates a Daily Log;
- Appoints the project management team;
- Identifies the type of solution to be provided (the project approach);
- Identifies the customer's quality expectations;
- Enters into the Daily Log any risks already known or discovered in the work of this process;
- Plans the initiation stage.

3.0.2 Why?

- To establish:
  - What is to be done?
  - Who will make the decisions?
  - Who is funding the project?

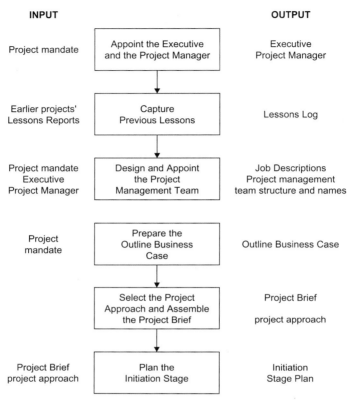

FIGURE 3.1   Starting up a Project.

- Who will say what is needed?
- What quality standards will be required?
- Who will provide the resources to do the work?

3.1 APPOINT THE EXECUTIVE AND PROJECT MANAGER

3.1.1 Responsibility

Corporate or programme management.

3.1.2 What Does the Activity Do?

- It appoints the Executive and Project Manager, prepares and signs their job descriptions.

3.1.3 Why?

Every project needs a sponsor, the key decision-maker. But normally this person is too busy to manage the project on a day-to-day basis. So we also need a Project Manager to do the planning and control. We need to identify these two people before anything can happen (in a controlled manner) in a project.

3.1.4 How?

- Corporate or programme management identifies the Executive to be responsible for the project.
- Either corporate/programme management or the Executive or both identify a suitable Project Manager.
- The Project Manager starts with the standard PRINCE2 role descriptions for the Executive and Project Manager positions. These are then tailored by discussion between the Executive and the Project Manager.
- The tailored roles are typed up; both people sign two copies of their job descriptions. The individual keeps one; the other is kept by the Project Manager for filing once the project filing system has been set up.

3.2 CAPTURE PREVIOUS LESSONS

3.2.1 Responsibility

Project Manager.

3.2.2 What Does the Activity Do?

- Creates a Lessons Log;
- Looks for lessons from previous similar projects that might be relevant to this project.

3.2.3 Why?

It would be foolish to ignore lessons that might help the project.

3.2.4 How?

- Such sources as quality assurance, programme management and other experienced Project Managers may have lessons that could avoid problems or provide good advice.
- Once PRINCE2 has been used for several projects, there will be Lessons Reports from these projects that may be useful.

3.3 DESIGN AND APPOINT THE PROJECT MANAGEMENT TEAM

3.3.1 Responsibility

Executive and Project Manager.

3.3.2 What Does the Activity Do?

- Proposes the other Project Board members;
- Discusses with the Project Board members whether they will need help to carry out their assurance responsibilities;
- Designs any Project Assurance roles to be delegated;
- Identifies candidates for any Project Assurance roles to be delegated;
- Identifies any required Team Managers; Team Manager names may not be known at this point and can be added later;
- Identifies any Project Support requirements.

3.3.3 Why?

The complete project management team needs to reflect the interests and have the approval of:

- Corporate/programme management;
- The users of the final product, those who will specify details of the required product;
- The supplier(s) of that product.

Project Board members must decide whether they want independent checks on their particular interests in the project as the project progresses (the Project Assurance part of the role) or whether they can do this verification themselves.

The Project Manager has to decide if any administrative support is needed, such as planning and control tool expertise, configuration management, filing or help with specialist techniques.

3.3.4 How?

- Identify customer areas that will use or control the end product, the commitment required and the level of authority and decision-making which is suitable for the criticality and size of the project (Senior User).
- Identify who will provide the end product(s) and the level of commitment and authority required from them (Senior Supplier).
- Identify candidates for the roles.
- Check out their availability and provisional agreement.
- Check whether the Project Board members will carry out their own Project Assurance responsibilities.
- Identify candidates for any Project Assurance functions which are to be delegated.
- Check out their availability.
- Consider whether any Team Managers will be required.
- Decide if any Project Support will be required.
- Identify resources for any required support.
- The project management team design is presented to corporate/ programme management for approval.
- The Project Manager discusses and agrees upon each member's job description with them based on the role descriptions found in Appendix B.

3.4 PREPARE THE OUTLINE BUSINESS CASE

3.4.1 Responsibility

Executive.

3.4.2 What Does the Activity Do?

- It begins the preparation of the Business Case from information either found in the project mandate or requested from corporate or programme management.
- At this point it may only be the reasons for the project that are known. Full financial justification will be developed during initiation.

3.4.3 Why?

PRINCE2 believes that a small amount of time and resource, relative to the likely cost of the project, should be spent in ensuring that the expense of the project is justified.

3.4.4 How?

The Executive

- Creates the outline Business Case, based on what is currently known about the project;
- Ensures understanding of the project reasons and objectives;
- Identifies how the project will contribute towards programme or corporate objectives;
- Understands how the project will be funded;
- Learns from any previous lessons on business justification;
- Where necessary, obtains approval of the outline Business Case from programme or corporate management.

The Project Manager

- Creates the Project Product Description;
- Identifies the customer's quality expectations;
- Agrees with the customer(s) what the project's acceptance criteria are;
- Checks the feasibility of any target date or cost mentioned in the project mandate or outline Business Case;

- Captures any risks identified while obtaining this information in the Daily Log;
- Summarizes any significant risks as part of the outline Business Case.

3.5 SELECT THE PROJECT APPROACH AND ASSEMBLE THE PROJECT BRIEF

3.5.1 Responsibility

Project Manager.

3.5.2 What Does the Activity Do?

- Project Brief
  - Identify all stakeholders – those with an interest in the project. Ensure their views are known on the following information.
  - Confirm project objectives and desired outcomes.
  - Confirm project scope (including any exclusions).
  - Identify any interfaces required of the project's products.
  - Identify project tolerances from programme or corporate management.
- Project Approach
  - Identify the operational environment in which the solution must work when delivered.
  - Decide what kind of a solution (project approach) will be provided to fit into that environment in order to achieve the points made in the outline Business Case and the general method of providing that solution.
  - Identify the skills required to implement the project approach.
  - Identify any timing implications of the project approach.

The main Project Approaches to be considered are:

- Build a solution from scratch.
- Take an existing product and modify it.

- Give the job to another organization to do for you.
- Buy a ready-made solution 'off the shelf'.

Finally, assemble the Project Brief.

3.5.3 Why?

The project approach will affect the timescale and cost of the project, plus possibly its control over scope and quality. This information should be made available to the Project Board in deciding whether or not to initiate the project.

A check should be made that the proposed project approach is in line with the customer's (or programme) strategy.

The Project Brief is the basis for the Project Board decision on whether or not to authorize initiation.

3.5.4 How?

- Identify any time, money, resource, operational support or later product extension constraints.
- Check for any direction or guidance on project approach from earlier documents such as the project mandate.
- Identify any security constraints.
- Check for any corporate/programme statement of direction which might constrain the choice of project approaches.
- Consider how the product might be brought into use and whether there are any problems that would impact the choice of the project approach.
- Produce a range of alternative project approaches.
- Identify the training needs of the alternatives.
- Compare the alternatives against the gathered information and constraints.
- Prepare a recommendation.
- Collate the Project Brief information (see above).
- Incorporate the outline Business Case.

- Incorporate the Project Product Description.
- Incorporate the project approach.
- Incorporate the project management team structure and role descriptions (or point to where these can be found).
- Record any new risks or issues in the Daily Log.

3.6 PLAN THE INITIATION STAGE

3.6.1 Responsibility

Project Manager.

3.6.2 What Does the Activity Do?

- It produces a plan for the initiation stage of the project.
  - If the initiation stage is to be of a significant size, the Project Manager should consider whether it would be sensible to use the 'Controlling a Stage' and 'Managing Product Delivery' processes to control the work.

3.6.3 Why?

Investigating and establishing the foundation of a project and then preparing a document to get an approval to start the project is important work. It needs planning, and since initiation will consume some resources, the Project Board should approve the plan.

3.6.4 How?

- Examine the Project Brief and decide how much work is needed in order to produce the Project Initiation Documentation.
- Evaluate the time needed to create the Project Plan.
- Evaluate the time needed to create the next Stage Plan.
- Evaluate the time needed to refine the Business Case.
- Evaluate the time needed to perform risk analysis.
- Create a plan for the initiation stage.
- Submit the initiation Stage Plan for Project Board approval.

Chapter 4

Initiating a Project (IP)

All activities are the responsibility of the Project Manager (Figure 4.1). Some, such as the creation of Configuration Item Records and the Issue Register, may be delegated to Project Support if the project is large enough to staff this role separately.

4.0.1 What Does the Process Do?

- Defines a strategy to cover the quality responsibilities, quality methods and tools to be used;

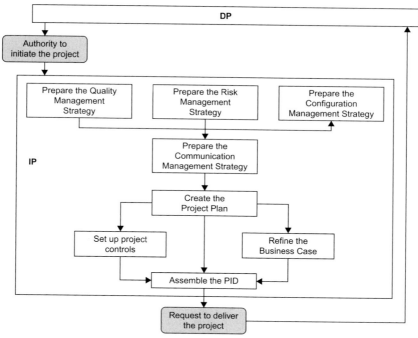

FIGURE 4.1   Initiating a project.

- Defines a strategy for how risks will be managed;
- Defines a strategy for how products and any changes to them will be controlled;
- Defines a strategy for communicating with all interested parties;
- Creates a high-level plan for the whole project;
- Identifies how the project is to be controlled;
- Expands and confirms the existence of a viable Business Case;
- Re-assesses the risks facing the project;
- Prepares documentation to ask the decision-makers to sign up to the project;
- Prepares the next Stage Plan.

4.0.2 Why?

All stakeholders with interest in the project should reach an agreement before major expenditure starts on what is to be done and why it is being done.

4.1 PREPARE THE QUALITY MANAGEMENT STRATEGY

4.1.1 What Does the Activity Do?

- Takes the quality expectations of the customer, the quality standards of both customer and supplier and the project approach, and defines how the quality expected by the customer will be achieved.

4.1.2 Why?

To be successful, the project must deliver a quality product as well as meet time and cost constraints. The means of achieving quality must be specified before the work begins.

Quality work cannot be planned until the quality expectations of the customer are known.

The time and cost of the project will be affected by the amount of quality work that has to be done; therefore, quality planning must be done before a realistic Project Plan can be produced.

4.1.3 How?

- Verify that the customer's quality expectations are understood.
- Establish links to any corporate or programme quality assurance function.
- Establish what the customer's quality standards are.
- Establish what the supplier quality standards are.
- Decide if there is a need for an independent quality assurance function to have representation on the project management team.
- Identify quality responsibilities for project products of both the customer and supplier in their job descriptions.
- Establish how quality will be achieved.
- Create the Quality Register.

4.2 PREPARE THE RISK MANAGEMENT STRATEGY

4.2.1 What Does the Activity Do?

- Describes the procedure to be used in handling risks;
- Identifies risk responsibilities;
- Defines any tools and techniques to be used in the management of risk;
- Describes any risk-reporting requirements.

4.2.2 Why?

Projects bring change, and therefore the possibility of risk is always present. Before a project begins, the method of identifying, analysing and controlling risks must be established.

4.2.3 How?

- Find out if there are any corporate or programme risk strategies, practices and standards that the project should use.
- Review the Lessons Log for any that relate to risk.
- Check if the Daily Log already has some risk entries.

- Create a Risk Management Strategy for the project, including:
  - Procedures to cover identifying, evaluating, assessing, coun-
    tering, monitoring and communicating;
  - Risk tools and techniques to be used;
  - Records to be kept;
  - Risk tolerances;
  - Responsibilities for risk activities.
- Check the Risk Management Strategy with Project Assurance to
  confirm that it meets the Project Board's needs.
- Create the Risk Register.
- Transfer any risks currently recorded in the Daily Log to the Risk
  Register.

4.3 PREPARE THE CONFIGURATION MANAGEMENT STRATEGY

4.3.1 What Does the Activity Do?

- Defines where and how project management and specialist
  products will be stored, how they will be identified and how
  access to them will be controlled;
- Defines how changes will be controlled.

4.3.2 Why?

A project must maintain control over the management and specialist products created and used. Time and money can be wasted if
people work from old copies that should have been withdrawn. A
product should be protected against unauthorized changes.

Changes are inevitable in any project, and can destroy plans, scope
of the project, quality, benefits, etc. unless carefully controlled.

4.3.3 How?

- Review any corporate or programme configuration management
  standards that should be used.

- Consider the project's needs for configuration management (in terms of the number of products there will be, project length and any security requirements).
- Check for any lessons about configuration management in the Lessons Log.
- Check the Risk Register for any risks concerning configuration management.
- Create a Configuration Management Strategy, including:
  - Product identification, control and what product status it is important to know;
  - How the accuracy of the records will be checked against the actual product states and versions;
  - Responsibilities – who will act as configuration librarian;
  - Change control procedure and records to be kept;
  - Change control responsibilities (e.g. Will there be a change authority? Should there be a change budget?).
- Create the Issue Register.
- Transfer any current issues that were previously recorded in the Daily Log.
- Check the Configuration Management Strategy with Project Assurance to ensure that it meets the needs of the Project Board.
- Create Configuration Item Records for the management products created so far.

4.4 PREPARE THE COMMUNICATION MANAGEMENT STRATEGY

4.4.1 What Does the Activity Do?

- Defines the communication lines internally within the project management team and externally with corporate or programme management, stakeholders and any other interested parties;
- Defines the timing of all communications and their content;
- Identifies the responsibilities for each communication.

4.4.2 Why?

Good communication between the relevant parties is a major benefit to a project. It avoids delays and misunderstandings.

4.4.3 How?

- Research any corporate or programme standard communication needs, formats and timings.
- Check for any lessons about communication in the Lessons Log.
- Discuss with the Project Board both its requirements for communication and the project's requirements for information from the Project Board.
- Identify all stakeholders and discuss with them their communication needs (remember that the Project Board is the source of all decisions and not the stakeholders).
- Check the Quality, Risk and Configuration Strategies for any communication needs.
- Create a Communication Management Strategy, including:
  - Procedures;
  - Formats;
  - Timings;
  - Responsibilities;
  - Tools and techniques.
- Check the strategy with Project Assurance to ensure that it will meet Project Board needs.
- If any risks or issues are created as a result of this work, update the appropriate register or the Daily Log.

4.5 CREATE THE PROJECT PLAN

4.5.1 What Does the Activity Do?

- Produces the Project Plan.

4.5.2 Why?

As part of its decision on whether or not to proceed with the project, the Project Board needs to know how much it is likely to cost and how long it will take. Details of the Project Plan also feed into the Business Case to indicate the viability of the project.

4.5.3 How?

- Understand from the Project Brief what the project has to deliver.
- Identify any corporate or programme standards or tools that have to be used.
- Discuss with the Project Board the format in which it wants the Project Plan to be produced.
- Understand the project approach to be taken.
- Check for any lessons in the Lessons Log that relate to planning.
- Create the Project Plan (ideally using the PRINCE2 product-based planning technique).
- Review the plan against any project (and particularly resource) constraints.
- Modify the plan accordingly.
- Check that the plan meets the requirements of the Quality, Risk and Configuration Management Strategies.
- Check the plan informally with Project Assurance.

4.6 SET UP THE PROJECT CONTROLS

4.6.1 What Does the Activity Do?

- Establishes control points for the project, based on the project's size, criticality, risk situation, the customer's and supplier's control standards and the diversity of stakeholders.

4.6.2 Why?

In order to keep the project under control it is important to ensure that:

- The right decisions are made by the right people at the right time.
- The right information is given to the right people at the right frequency and timing.

4.6.3 How?

- Check the Project Brief for corporate or programme standards for project control.
- Check for any lessons in the Lessons Log on project control.
- Check the Risk and Issue Registers for anything that might affect project control.
- Ensure that role descriptions define all decision-making authorities and responsibilities.
- Agree on a suitable breakdown of the project into stages with the Project Board.
- Agree on the format of reports to the Project Board and the stakeholders.
- Agree on the frequency of the Project Board and stakeholder reports.
- Establish reporting requirements from team(s) to the Project Manager.
- Check that there are sufficient risk and Business Case monitoring activities in the plans.

4.7 REFINE THE BUSINESS CASE (*AND RISKS*)

4.7.1 What Does the Activity Do?

- Takes whatever outline Business Case exists for the project, plus the Project Plan, and creates a full Business Case for inclusion in the Project Initiation Documentation;

- Carries out a further risk analysis and management for the project based on the new information created;
- Creates the Benefits Review Plan.

4.7.2 Why?

Before commitment to the project it is important to ensure that there is sufficient justification for the resource expenditure and that there is a sound balance between business justification and the risks.

4.7.3 How?

- If a Business Case was included in the project mandate, check if its circumstances and assumptions have changed.
- Investigate the work reasons for the project with the customer.
- Investigate the business reasons for the project with the Executive.
- Quantify the benefits wherever possible.
- Incorporate the costs from the Project Plan.
- Review the Lessons Log for lessons from other projects on refinement of the Business Case.
- Identify how achievement of each benefit is to be measured.
- Take baseline measures of the current situation of each benefit area against which achievement can be measured.
- Identify when benefits should have been achieved so that benefit reviews can be planned.
- Update the Risk Register with any new or changed risks.
- Modify the Project Plan to reflect any changes caused by risk analysis.

4.8 ASSEMBLE THE PROJECT INITIATION DOCUMENTATION

4.8.1 What Does the Activity Do?

- Gathers together the information from the other IP activities and assembles the Project Initiation Documentation;

- Prepares a plan for the next stage (see the *Managing a Stage Boundary* process).

4.8.2 Why?

The Project Initiation Documentation encapsulates all the information needed for the Project Board to make the decision on whether or not to go ahead with the project. It also forms a formal record of the information on which the decision was based, and can be used after the project finishes in order to judge how successful the project was.

If the Project Board makes a general decision to proceed with the project, it needs to have more detailed information about the cost and duration of the next stage before committing the required resources.

4.8.3 How?

- Assemble the required information.
- Decide how best to present the information.
- Create the Project Initiation Documentation.
- Invoke the *Managing a Stage Boundary* process to produce the next Stage Plan.
- Check that the plan meets the requirements of the Quality Management Strategy.
- Distribute the two documents to the Project Board, others with Project Assurance roles and stakeholders.

Chapter 5

Directing a Project (DP)

All activities are the responsibility of the Project Board (Figure 5.1). Production of many of the products will be delegated.

5.0.1 What Does the Process Do?

- Authorizes project initiation;
- Authorizes the project;
- Provides liaison with corporate/programme management;
- Advises the Project Manager of any external business events which might impact the project;
- Approves Stage Plans;
- Approves stage closure;
- Decides on any changes to approved products;
- Approves any Exception Plans;
- Gives ad hoc advice and direction throughout the project;
- Safeguards the interests of the customer and the supplier;
- Approves project closure.

5.0.2 Why?

Day-to-day management is left to the Project Manager, but the Project Board must exercise overall control and make the key decisions.

5.1 AUTHORIZE INITIATION

5.1.1 What Does the Activity Do?

- Checks that adequate terms of reference exist;

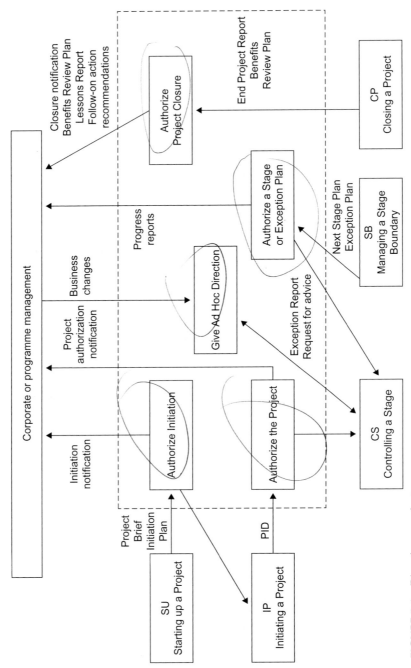

FIGURE 5.1 Directing a project.

- Checks and approves the initiation Stage Plan;
- Commits the resources required to carry out the initiation stage work.

5.1.2 Why?

The initiation stage confirms that a viable project exists and that everybody concerned agrees on what is to be done. Like all project work, the effort to do this needs the approval of the Project Board.

5.1.3 How?

- Confirm the terms of reference in the Project Brief, checking if necessary with corporate/programme management.
- Review and approve the Project Product Description.
- Confirm the customer's quality expectations and acceptance criteria.
- Check whether the outline Business Case shows that there are valid reasons to authorize initiation at least.
- Confirm that the recommended project approach is suitable.
- Formally approve appointments to the project management team and confirm that everyone has an agreed role description.
- Check the initiation Stage Plan and approve it if satisfied.
- Agree upon tolerance margins for the initiation stage.
- Agree upon control and reporting arrangements for the initiation stage.
- Inform all stakeholders that initiation has been authorized and request any support required from them for initiation.
- Commit the resources required by the plan.

5.2 AUTHORIZE THE PROJECT

5.2.1 What Does the Activity Do?

- Decides whether to proceed with the rest of the project or not;
- Approves the next Stage Plan.

5.2.2 Why?

The activity gives the Project Board a decision point before major resource commitment to the project.

5.2.3 How?

- Confirm that the project's objectives and scope are clearly defined and understood by all.
- Confirm that the objectives are in line with corporate/programme objectives.
- Confirm that all authorities and responsibilities are agreed upon.
- Confirm that the Business Case is adequate, clear and, wherever possible, measurable.
- Confirm that any useful lessons from previous projects have been incorporated.
- Confirm the existence of a credible Project Plan which is within the project constraints.
- Check that the proposed project controls are prepared and are suitable for the type and size of the project.
- Confirm that the Quality, Risk, Configuration and Communication Strategies are prepared and provide adequate management and control over their areas.
- Confirm that tolerance levels for the project have been set by corporate or programme management and are realistic.
- Check that the Benefits Review Plan is established, covers all the expected benefits and provides details of how and when each benefit will be measured.
- Make any desired changes to the draft Project Initiation Documentation.
- Check that the plan for the next stage is reasonable and matches that portion of the Project Plan.
- Establish the tolerances for the next stage.
- Give written approval for the next stage (or not, if unhappy with any of the details).
- Arrange a date for the next stage's end stage assessment.
- Notify all stakeholders that the project has been authorized.

5.3 AUTHORIZE A STAGE OR EXCEPTION PLAN

5.3.1 What Does the Activity Do?

- The activity authorizes each stage (except initiation) and any Exception Plans that are needed.

5.3.2 Why?

An important control for the Project Board is to approve only one stage at a time. At the end of one stage, the Project Manager has to justify both progress so far and the plan for the next stage before being allowed to continue.

5.3.3 How?

- Compare the results of the current stage against the approved Stage Plan.
- Assess progress against the Project Plan.
- Assess the acceptability of the next Stage Plan against the Project Plan.
- Review the prospects of achieving the Business Case.
- Review the risks facing the project.
- Get direction from corporate/programme management if the project is forecasted to exceed tolerances or there is a significant change to the Business Case.
- Review tolerances for the next stage.
- Review reporting arrangements for the next stage.
- Give approval to move into the next stage (if satisfied).

5.4 GIVE AD HOC DIRECTION

5.4.1 What Does the Activity Do?

- Advises the Project Manager about any external events that impact the project;
- Gives direction to the Project Manager when asked for advice or a decision about an issue;
- Advises on or approves any changes to the project management team;

- Makes decisions on the actions to take on receipt of any Exception Reports.

5.4.2 Why?

There may be a need for occasional and immediate Project Board direction outside end-stage assessments.

5.4.3 How?

- Check for external events, such as business changes, that might affect the project's Business Case or risk exposure and keep the Project Manager aware of this information.
- Respond to any requests for advice and guidance from the Project Manager.
- Monitor any allocated risk situations.
- Check on the status of the stage by reviewing Highlight Reports.
- Make decisions on any Exception Reports.
- Make decisions on any requests for concessions where a product is not fully meeting its specification.
- Ensure that the project remains focused on its objectives and achievement of its Business Case.
- Keep corporate/programme management and stakeholders informed of project progress.
- Ask for any required advice or direction from corporate or programme management.
- Make decisions about any necessary changes to the project management team.
- Make decisions on Issue Reports brought to the attention of the Project Board.

5.5 AUTHORIZE PROJECT CLOSURE

5.5.1 What Does the Activity Do?

- Checks that the objectives of the project have been met;
- Checks that there are no loose ends;

- Discuss the Work Package with the Team Manager.
- Jointly assess any risks or problems and modify the Work Package and Risk Register as necessary.
- Review the Team Plan to ensure that sufficient resources and time have been allocated for the work.
- Verify sensible tolerances for the Work Package are within the stage tolerances. Quality tolerances are in the Product Descriptions, but time, cost and scope tolerances should be defined.
- Record the agreement of the Team Manager in the Work Package.
- Update the Stage Plan with any adjustments made as part of the agreement.
- Update the relevant Configuration Item Records to reflect their allocation.
- Update the Quality Register with details of agreed additional quality checking activities and resources.
- Update the Risk Register with any new or changed risks.

6.2 REVIEW WORK PACKAGE STATUS ✕

6.2.1 What Does the Activity Do?

- Gathers information to update the Stage Plan to reflect actual progress, effort expended and quality work carried out.

6.2.2 Why?

In order to control the stage and make sensible decisions on what, if any, adjustments need to be made, it is necessary to gather information on what has actually happened and be able to compare this against what was planned.

6.2.3 How?

- Collect Checkpoint Reports.
- Collect Team Plan progress information.

- Obtain estimates on time, cost and effort needed to complete work that is in progress.
- Check whether sufficient resources are available to complete the work as now estimated.
- Check the Quality Register for feedback on quality activities.
- Check that the Configuration Item Records reflect changes in the status of the Work Package products.
- Note any potential or real problems.
- Update the Risk and Issue Registers if required.
- Update the Stage Plan with the information.

6.3 CAPTURE AND EXAMINE ISSUES AND RISKS

For issues:

6.3.1 What Does the Activity Do?

- Makes a note in the Daily Log of any issues that can be dealt with by the Project Manager informally.
- Captures, logs and categorizes new Issue Reports.
- Analyses each new issue and recommends a course of action.
- Reviews each open issue for any change to its circumstances or impact and potentially makes a new recommendation.
- Reviews all open issues for any impact on the project risks or the Business Case.

6.3.2 Why?

At any time during the project a problem may occur, a change may be requested or the answer to a question may be sought. If these are missed, it may happen that the project fails to deliver what is required. Alternatively, the project may run into some other trouble that could have been foreseen, had the issue been noted at the time it arose. There must be a process to capture these so that they can be presented for the appropriate decision and response.

Having captured all issues, these should be examined for impact and the appropriate body for any extra information and decision identified.

6.3.3 How?

- Ensure that all possible sources of issues are being monitored.
- Enter issues that can be dealt with informally in the Daily Log.
- New issues are entered into the Issue Register.
- Assemble all pertinent information about the issue.
- Carry out impact analysis on the technical effort required to resolve the issue.
- Update the Risk Register if the issue reveals a new risk or a change to a known risk.
- Assess whether the issue or its resolution would impact the Business Case.
- Prepare a recommended course of action.
- Update the Issue Register with the impact analysis result.
- Record the issue formally on an Issue Report.

For risks:

6.3.4 What Does the Activity Do?

- Enters the risk in the Risk Register.
- Assesses the risk.

6.3.5 Why?

Like an issue, a risk may arise at any time. The situation should be monitored constantly for new risks and for changes in existing risks.

6.3.6 How?

- Ensure that all possible sources of risk are being monitored.
- Enter new risks on the Risk Register.
- Perform risk analysis on the risk.
- Assess whether a new risk or its resolution would impact the Stage Plan, the Project Plan and the Business Case.
- Review existing risks for any change.
- Plan selected responses.

- Check the Risk Management Strategy and Communication Management Strategy for any reporting needs.
- Enter any new risks on the Risk Register.
- Identify the risk event with its cause and effect.
- Assess the risk against the Stage and Project Plans and the Business Case and plan the selected response.

6.4 REVIEW STAGE STATUS

6.4.1 What Does the Activity Do?

- Provides a regular re-assessment of the status of the stage;
- Triggers new work;
- Triggers corrective action for any problems;
- Provides the information for progress reporting.

6.4.2 Why?

It is better to check the status of a stage on a regular basis and take action to avoid potential problems than have problems come as a surprise and then have to react to them.

6.4.3 How?

- Review Checkpoint Reports.
- Check the status of quality checks.
- Review progress against the Stage Plan.
- Where useful, request a Product Status Account to verify that records and actual progress match.
- Review resource and money expenditure.
- Review the impact of any implemented issues on Stage and Project Plans.
- Assess if the stage and project will remain within tolerances.
- Check the continuing validity of the Business Case.
- Check for changes in the status of any risks.
- Check for any changes external to the project which may impact it.
- Check the Benefits Review Plan to see if any benefit reviews are due and, if so, carry them out.

6.5 REPORT HIGHLIGHTS

6.5.1 What Does the Activity Do?

- Produces Highlight Reports for the Project Board.

6.5.2 Why?

The Project Board and stakeholders need to be kept informed of project progress if they are to exercise proper control over the project. Rather than have regular progress meetings, reports at regular intervals are recommended between assessments at the end of each stage. The Project Board decides the frequency of the reports during project initiation.

6.5.3 How?

- Collate the information from any Checkpoint Reports made since the last Highlight Report.
- Identify any significant Stage Plan revisions made since the last report.
- Identify any current or potential risks to the Business Case.
- Identify any change to other risks.
- Assess the Issue Register for any potential problems that require Project Board's attention.
- Review the previous Highlight Report for what was claimed would be done in this period.
- Prepare a Highlight Report for the Project Board, including a review of the progress forecast in the previous Highlight Report.

6.6 TAKE CORRECTIVE ACTION

6.6.1 What Does the Activity Do?

- Within the limits of the tolerance margins established by the Project Board, the Project Manager takes action to remedy any problems that arise.

6.6.2 Why?

Failing to take action when the project is drifting away from the Stage Plan invites loss of control.

6.6.3 How?

- Assemble information about any deviation from the plan.
- Identify possible solutions.
- Obtain any necessary advice from the Project Board on the proposed corrective actions.
- Create new Work Packages or amend existing ones to reflect the corrective actions.
- Update, where necessary, the Stage Plan, Configuration Item Records, Issue Reports, Issue and Risk Registers with the action taken.

6.7 ESCALATE ISSUES AND RISKS

6.7.1 What Does the Activity Do?

- Where an issue or risk threatens to go beyond tolerances and the Project Manager feels that he/she cannot take corrective action within the authority limits imposed by the Project Board, the situation must be brought to the attention of the Project Board for advice.

6.7.2 Why?

Part of the concept of management by exception is that the Project Manager will bring to the immediate attention of the Project Board anything that can be forecast to drive the plan outside the tolerance limits agreed upon with the Project Board. This is part of the Project Board staying in overall control.

6.7.3 How?

- Review the impact analysis of the deviation.
- Identify and evaluate options for recovery.

- Select a recommendation.
- Send an Exception Report to the Project Board detailing the problem.

6.8 RECEIVE COMPLETED WORK PACKAGES

6.8.1 What Does the Activity Do?

- Records the completion and return of approved Work Packages.

6.8.2 Why?

Where work has been recorded as approved to a team or individual, there should be a matching activity to record the return of the completed product(s) and its(their) acceptance (or otherwise).

6.8.3 How?

- Check the delivery against the requirements of the Work Package.
- Check that quality activities (if any) have been completed satisfactorily.
- Check that the recipients have accepted the products.
- Ensure that the delivered products have been baselined.
- Document any relevant team member appraisal information.
- Pass information about completion to update the Stage Plan.

Chapter 7

Managing Product Delivery (MP)

All activities are the responsibility of the Team Manager (Figure 7.1).

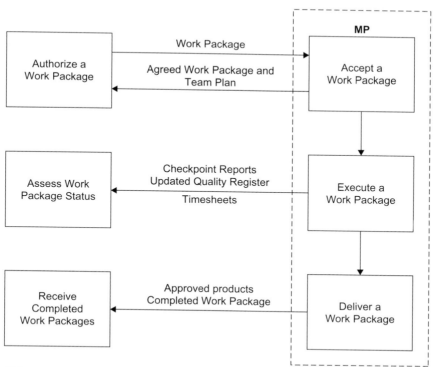

FIGURE 7.1   Managing product delivery.

7.0.1 What Does the Process Do?

- Agrees upon work requirements with the Project Manager;
- Does the work;
- Keeps the Project Manager informed on progress, quality and any problems;
- Gets approval for the finished work;
- Notifies the Project Manager that the work is finished.

7.0.2 Why?

- Where the Project Manager delegates work, there must be appropriate steps by the team or person to whom the work is delegated to indicate understanding and acceptance of the work. While the work is being done, there may be a need to report progress and confirm quality checking. When the work is complete, there should be an agreed way of confirming the satisfactory completion.

7.1 ACCEPT A WORK PACKAGE

7.1.1 What Does the Activity Do?

- Agrees upon the details of a Work Package with the Project Manager;
- Plans the work necessary to complete the Work Package.

7.1.2 Why?

There must be understanding and agreement between a Team Manager (or an individual) and the Project Manager on any delegated work.

7.1.3 How?

- Agree with the Project Manager on what is to be delivered.
- Ensure that the quality requirements are clear.

- Identify any independent people who must be involved in quality checking.
- Identify any target dates and/or constraints for the work.
- Identify any reporting requirements.
- Understand how the products of the Work Package are to be handed over when complete.
- Make a Team Plan to do the work.
- Assess the Team Plan for risks.
- Adjust the plan or negotiate a change to the Work Package so that the Work Package is achievable within the agreed constraints.
- Agree upon suitable tolerance margins for the Work Package.

7.2 EXECUTE A WORK PACKAGE

7.2.1 What Does the Activity Do?

- Manages the development/supply of the products/services defined in the Work Package.

7.2.2 Why?

Having agreed and committed to work, this activity covers the management of that work until its completion.

7.2.3 How?

- Allocate work to team members.
- Capture and record the effort expended.
- Ensure that the work is done according to the techniques, processes and procedures specified in the Work Package.
- Monitor progress against the tolerances agreed to for the work.
- Monitor and control the risks.
- Evaluate progress and the amount of effort still required to complete the product(s) of the Work Package.
- Feed progress reports back to the Project Manager at the frequency agreed upon in the Work Package.

- Ensure that the required quality checks are carried out.
- Ensure that the personnel identified in the Quality Register are involved in the quality checking.
- Update the Quality Register with results of all quality checks.
- Raise issues and/or risks to advise the Project Manager of any problems.
- Ensure that any changes to the status of a product are notified to the configuration librarian, so that Configuration Item Records are maintened correctly.

7.3 DELIVER A WORK PACKAGE

7.3.1 What Does the Activity Do?

- Obtains approval of the products developed/supplied;
- Delivers the products to whoever is responsible for configuration management;
- Advises the Project Manager of the completion of the work.

7.3.2 Why?

There has to be an activity to deliver the requested product(s) and document the agreement that the work has been done satisfactorily.

7.3.3 How?

- Confirm that the Quality Register has been updated with details of a successful check on the quality of the product(s).
- Confirm that the Configuration Item Records for the Work Package products reflect the completed status.
- Obtain approval from whoever is defined in the Work Package that the package is complete.
- Transfer the products and control of their release to the project's Configuration Librarian.
- Advise the Project Manager that the Work Package is complete.

Chapter 8

Managing a Stage Boundary (SB)

All activities are the responsibility of the Project Manager (Figure 8.1).

8.0.1 What Does the Process Do?

- Confirms to the Project Board that products planned to be produced in the current stage plan have been delivered;

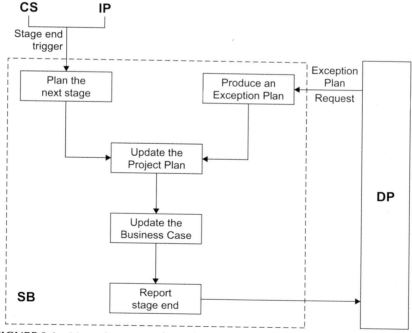

FIGURE 8.1 Managing a stage boundary.

- Gives reasons for the non-delivery of any products which were planned (in the case of deviation forecasts);
- Verifies that any useful lessons learned during the current stage have been recorded in the Lessons Log;
- Provides information to the Project Board to allow it to assess the continued viability of the project;
- Obtains approval for the next Stage Plan or the Exception Plan;
- Ascertains the tolerance margins to be applied to the new plan.

8.0.2 Why?

The ability to authorize a project to move forward a stage at a time is a major control for the Project Board. There is also a need for a process to create a plan to react to a forecast deviation beyond tolerances. This process aims to provide the information needed by the Project Board about the current status of the Project Plan, the Business Case and the risks to judge the continuing worth of the project and the commitment to a new plan.

8.1 PLAN THE NEXT STAGE

8.1.1 What Does the Activity Do?

- Prepares a plan for the next stage.

8.1.2 Why?

In order to adequately control a stage, the Project Manager needs a plan in which the detailed activities go down to the level of a handful of days.

8.1.3 How?

- Check the Project Initiation Documentation for any changes to acceptance criteria.
- Check the project approach for any changes and guidance on how the products of the next stage are to be produced.

- Check the Issue Register for any issues which may affect the next Stage Plan.
- Check the Risk Register for any risks which may affect the next Stage Plan.
- Check the Quality Management Strategy for the quality standards to be used.
- Create the next Stage Plan.
- Create or update any Configuration Item Records required for the next stage.
- Document any changes to the personnel of the project management team.
- Discuss the draft plan with those who have Project Assurance responsibilities.
- Add any formal quality reviews and any other quality checks required for Project Assurance purposes to the Quality Register.
- Identify (as a minimum) the chair of each formal quality review.
- Identify the required reviewer skills and authority required for each formal quality review with those with Project Assurance responsibilities.
- Ensure that the plan includes all required management products.
- Check the plan for any new or changed risks and update the Risk Register.
- Modify the plan, if necessary, in the light of risk analysis.
- Create contingency plans for any serious risks that cannot be avoided or reduced to manageable proportions.

8.2 UPDATE THE PROJECT PLAN

8.2.1 What Does the Activity Do?

- Updates the Project Plan with the actual costs and schedule from the stage that has just finished, plus the estimated costs and schedule of the next Stage Plan.

8.2.2 Why?

As one stage is completed and the next one planned, the Project Plan must be updated so that the Project Board has the most up-to-date information on the likely project costs and schedule on which to partially base its decision on whether the project is still a viable business proposition.

8.2.3 How?

- Ensure that the current Stage Plan has been updated with final costs and dates.
- Create a new version of the Project Plan ready to be updated.
- Update the new version of the Project Plan with the actual costs and dates of the current stage.
- Update the Project Plan with the estimated costs, resource requirements and dates of the next Stage Plan or the Exception Plan.
- Update any later stages of the Project Plan on the basis of any relevant information made available since the last update.
- Check to see if events indicate that the Project Initiation Documentation has to be modified.
- Update the Issue and/or Risk Registers if new issues or risks have been identified or existing ones need to be modified.

8.3 UPDATE THE BUSINESS CASE

8.3.1 What Does the Activity Do?

- Modifies the Business Case, where appropriate, on the basis of information from the current stage and the plan for the next stage;
- Checks the known risks to project success for any change to their circumstances and looks for any new risks.

8.3.2 Why?

The whole project should be business-driven, so the Project Board should review a revised Business Case as a major part of the check on the continued viability of the project.

Part of the assessment of the project's viability is an examination of the likelihood and impact of potential risks.

8.3.3 How?

- Create a new version of the Business Case ready to be updated.
- Review the expected costs in the investment appraisal against the new forecast in the updated Project Plan.
- Review the financial benefits in the investment appraisal against any new forecasts.
- Review the goals in the Business Case and check that there has been no change or that no new goals have come to light.
- Ensure that the Risk Register is up-to-date with the latest information on the identified risks.
- Modify the new version of the Business Case in light of any changes to the forecast.
- Ensure that the Benefits Review Plan has been updated with the results of any benefit reviews carried out during the stage.
- Ensure that the Benefits Review Plan reflects any changes to the Business Case.
- Update the Risk and Issue Registers if required.

8.4 REPORT STAGE END

8.4.1 What Does the Activity Do?

- Reports on the results of the current stage or the situation that caused the creation of an Exception Plan;
- Forecasts the time and resource requirements of the next stage, if applicable;
- Looks for a Project Board decision on the future of the project.

8.4.2 Why?

Normally the Project Board manages by exception and therefore only needs to meet if things are forecast to deviate beyond tolerance levels. But as part of its control, the Project Board only gives approval to the Project Manager to undertake one stage at a time, at the end of which it reviews the anticipated benefits, costs, timescales and risks and makes a decision whether to continue with the project. This situation also arises if the Project Board has requested the creation of an Exception Report.

8.4.3 How?

- Report the actual costs and time of the current stage and measure these against the plan which was approved by the Project Board.
- Report the impact of the current stage's costs and time taken on the Project Plan.
- Report any impact from the current stage's results on the Business Case, including any benefits realized during the stage.
- Consider (in long projects) whether the production of a Lessons Report at this point would be of value to corporate or programme management.
- Report the status of the Issue Register.
- Report the extent and results of the quality work done in the current stage.
- Provide details of the next Stage Plan (if applicable) or Exception Plan.
- Identify any necessary revisions to the Project Plan caused by the next Stage Plan.
- Identify any changes to the Business Case caused by the next Stage Plan.
- Report the risk situation.
- Recommend the next action (e.g. approval of the next Stage Plan).

8.5 PRODUCE AN EXCEPTION PLAN

8.5.1 What Does the Activity Do?

- In response to an Exception Report, the Project Board may request the Project Manager to prepare a new plan to replace the remainder of the current plan.

8.5.2 Why?

The Project Board approves a Stage Plan on the understanding that it stays within its defined tolerance margins. When an Exception Report indicates that the current tolerances are likely to be exceeded, the Project Board may ask for a new plan to reflect that the changed situation can be controlled within newly specified tolerance margins. The Project Board may take other measures, such as premature closure of the project or removal of the problem causing the deviation.

8.5.3 How?

- An Exception Plan has exactly the same format as a Stage Plan. Section 8.1.3 defines the actions needed to develop a Stage Plan, which can be followed for an Exception Plan.
- An Exception Plan covers the time from the present moment to the end of the plan that is to be replaced.

Chapter 9

Closing a Project (CP)

All activities are the responsibility of the Project Manager (Figure 9.1). Work may be delegated to Project Support.

9.0.1 What Does the Process Do?

- Checks that all required products have been delivered and accepted;
- Checks that the products can be maintained and supported after the project disbands;
- Checks that all issues have been dealt with;
- Records any recommendations for subsequent work on the product;
- Recognizes that the project has nothing more to contribute (possibly a premature close);
- Reviews project performance against what it set out to do;
- Passes on any lessons from the project;
- Recommends closure of the project to the Project Board;
- Updates plans to measure the achievement of the project's benefits (Figure 9.1).

9.0.2 Why?

Every project should come to a controlled completion.

In order to have its success measured, a project must be brought to a close when the Project Manager believes that it has met the objectives set out in the project contract.

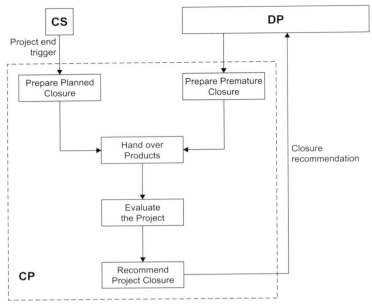

FIGURE 9.1   Closing a project.

9.1 PREPARE PLANNED CLOSURE

9.1.1 What Does the Activity Do?

- Produces the final picture of the project cost and duration;
- Gets agreement from the customer that the acceptance criteria have been met;
- Confirms acceptance of the project's final product from the customer and those who will support the product during its operational life;
- Prepares notification of project closure for the Project Board to send to corporate or programme management.

9.1.2 Why?

The customer and the supplier must agree that a project has met its objectives before it can close.

The Project Board will need to know the results and the final costs of the project.

9.1.3 How?

- Update the Project Plan with figures from the final Stage Plan.
- Review the Project Product Description with the customer and get the customer's agreement that the acceptance criteria have been met.
- Obtain a Product Status Account to confirm that all products have been completed and accepted by the customer.
- Prepare notification of project closure for the Project Board to send to corporate or programme management to confirm that project resources can be released.

9.2 PREPARE PREMATURE CLOSURE

9.2.1 What Does the Activity Do?

- Ensures that any useful products created so far have been handed over to the customer;
- Reviews the state of any unfinished products for risk situations that they may cause or maintenance work that will be required after the project has closed.

9.2.2 Why?

For a number of reasons the Project Board may instruct the Project Manager to bring a project to a premature close. In such circumstances, the work done so far should not be thrown away. An effort should be made to salvage any products created so far, and any risks or gaps left by the uncompleted project should be brought to the attention of the Project Board for it to pass on.

9.2.3 How?

- Update the Project Plan with figures from the final Stage Plan.
- Obtain a Product Status Account and determine which products:
  1. Have already been accepted;
  2. May be useful to other projects;

3. Have been started and need to be finished;
4. Are covered by concessions;
5. Need to be made safe and secure.
6. Have not been started.
- From the above list, discuss with the Project Board any completion work that is needed and, if necessary, create a suitable Exception Plan.
- Check the Issue Register for any issues which should be transferred to the follow-on action recommendations.
- Check the Risk Register for any risks that may affect those products that were completed in their operational life and add these to the follow-on action recommendations.
- Identify if measurement can be made of any of the original planned benefits and, if so, prepare a plan to carry out that measurement.
- Perform a reduced version of the other closure activities.

9.3 HAND-OVER PRODUCTS

9.3.1 What Does the Activity Do?

- Identifies any work which should be done following the project;
- Prepares a plan for when the realization of the project's expected benefits should be checked;
- Checks that all issues are closed;
- Arranges archiving for the project files.

9.3.2 Why?

Any knowledge of unfinished business at the end of a project should be documented, checked with the Project Board and passed to the appropriate body for action.

There must be a check that there are no outstanding problems or requests.

The project documentation, particularly agreements and approvals, should be preserved for any later audits.

9.3.3 How?

- Hand over the project's products to the operations and maintenance organizations as defined in the Configuration Management Strategy. Confirm acceptance from the operations and maintenance organizations of the hand-over.
- Check for any omissions in the product or suggestions on how to improve the product and put these on the follow-on action recommendations.
- Ensure that the omissions and suggestions are recorded as follow-on action recommendations.
- Check the Issue Register for any issues which were not completed or rejected and transfer them to the follow-on action recommendations.
- Check the Risk Register for any risks that may affect the product in its operational life and add these to the follow-on action recommendations.
- Check that the Benefits Review Plan is up-to-date and shows how and when all benefits that will be achieved during the final product's operational life will be achieved.

9.4 EVALUATE THE PROJECT

9.4.1 What Does the Activity Do?

- Assesses the project's results against its objectives;
- Provides statistics on the performance of the project;
- Records useful lessons that were learned.

9.4.2 Why?

One way in which to improve the quality of project management is to learn from the lessons of past projects.

As part of closing the project, the Project Board needs to assess the performance of the project and the Project Manager. This may also form a part of the customer's appraisal of a supplier, to see if the contract has been completed or to see if that supplier should be used again.

9.4.3 How?

- Compare the project's achievements and performance against the original Project Initiation Documentation and the latest version of it.
- Write the End Project Report, evaluating the management, quality and technical methods, tools and processes used.
- Add to the End Project Report any follow-on action recommendations (see the *Hand Over Products* activity).
- Complete the Lessons Report from the following:
  1. Examine the Risk Register and actions taken, and record any useful comments.
  2. Examine the Issue Register and actions taken, and record any useful comments.
  3. Examine the Quality Register and record any useful comments.

9.5 RECOMMEND PROJECT CLOSURE

9.5.1 What Does the Activity Do?

- Once the Project Manager can confirm that the project can be closed, a closure recommendation should be sent to the Project Board.

9.5.2 Why?

The Project Board should receive confirmation that everything has been finished before it informs corporate or programme management. It is the Project Board's responsibility to release project resources and advise suppliers of the need to submit final invoices.

9.5.3 How?

- Ensure that the Issue, Quality and Risk Registers and the Lessons Log have been closed.
- Write the End Project Report, evaluating the management, quality and technical methods, tools and processes used.
- Complete and archive the project files.
- Provide the Project Board with a project closure notification for it to forward to corporate or programme management. The Communications Management Strategy should be consulted to find others who should be notified of project closure.

Chapter 10

Business Case

10.1 PHILOSOPHY

Every project should be driven by a business need. If it has no justification in terms of the business, it should not be undertaken. If the justification disappears, the project should be stopped.

The Business Case is a vital project management tool. It should be considered before any project is commissioned, ideally at a higher level such as the strategy group, and certainly as part of any feasibility study.

In a customer/supplier environment it is likely that both parties will have their own Business Case; the customer looking for benefits to be obtained from the result of the project, the supplier looking to make a profit from the development work. PRINCE2 concentrates on the customer's Business Case.

10.2 HOW?

An outline Business Case should be included in the project mandate. If it is not, then one should be added as part of developing the Project Brief.

If a project is part of a larger programme, its justification will point at the Business Case of the programme. In such a case, the project may have no business justification itself, but contribute to achievement of the programme Business Case. In this case, the project Business

Case will refer back to the continuing need for the project within the perceived needs for the programme.

10.3 WHO?

The official PRINCE2 manual can seem quite confusing about responsibilities for the Business Case and who does what and when. Here is a set of bullets that will clarify, hopefully, the various points:

- In some cases there may be a predefined Business Case in the project mandate set out by corporate management or by programme management if the project is part of a programme.
- The Business Case is the responsibility of the Executive from *Starting up a Project* until the project closes. If there is not an outline of the Business Case in the project mandate, it is the Executive's job to get it.
- The Executive will often ask for the Project Manager's help in preparing the Business Case.
- Project Assurance may assist in the development of the Business Case, ensure that it fits corporate strategy and monitor it against project progress and external events.
- The Senior User(s) is responsible for specifying to the Executive what the benefits will be and providing measurements of today's situation against which benefit realization can be measured once the products are in use.
- Once the project finishes, responsibility for the Benefits Review Plan passes to corporate or programme management.
- The Senior User(s) will be asked by corporate or programme management to provide measurements of benefits realization according to the Benefits Review Plan.
- Different benefits may take different lengths of time to appear. Therefore, there may be more than one benefit review.

10.4 WHEN?

The Business Case should be formally reviewed at the start of a project, and again at stage boundaries and at project closure.

It should also be reviewed when major change requests are made. It should be monitored continuously throughout the project.

10.5 CONTENT

10.5.1 Reasons

This is a narrative description of the justification for undertaking the project.

10.5.2 Business Options

What were the business options, the selected option and reasons for its selection?

PRINCE2 offers a guide that business options should be considered under three headings:

The 'do nothing' option
    The first option always to be considered is to do nothing, to simply carry on as before. What costs will be avoided? What benefits will be lost? Will the company be able to cope if it does not 'do something'?
    It is important to remember that the 'do nothing' option should be calculated by assessing the implications of staying with the current mode of operation for the anticipated life of the new product/service/system.
The 'do something' option
    Estimates of the implications of implementing a variety of solutions need to be made in a similar way and over a similar time period to the 'do nothing' option above.
The 'do the minimum' option
    As the title suggests, this is a question of what bare minimum could be done to solve the business problem.

The choice between the three types is a matter of weighing the benefits and savings against costs.

It should be made clear at this point that business options are not the same as the project approach. Here is an example. The business problem might have been a fall in profits in a subsidiary company. The options might have been:

- Do nothing.
- Close down the subsidiary.
- Trim the workforce.
- Improve the marketing of the subsidiary's products.

Say the last one is the selected option, the project approach would be how to deliver the improved marketing.

10.5.3 Expected Benefits

This is a description of what the expected benefits are plus estimated benefit figures over the life of the product. Benefits should be defined in terms that are:

- Measurable at the start of the project;
- Measurable when the final product is in use.

10.5.4 Negative Effects

Are there any disadvantages of the proposed business solution? (The PRINCE2 manual uses a non-English word, 'dis-benefits', for this.)

10.5.5 Costs

They are the estimated development and running costs for the product.

10.5.6 Timescale

This is the estimated duration of the project and the timescale required before the benefits can be realized.

10.5.7 Major Risks

This is a summary of any major risks, their likely impact and contingency plans (including their cost), should they occur.

10.5.8 Investment Appraisal

This considers what would happen if the project was not done – none of the costs would be incurred and the benefits would not be accrued. This is known as the 'do nothing' option and is used as the benchmark against which the predicted costs and benefits are measured.

10.6 BENEFITS REVIEW PLAN

The concept of justifying a project through a Business Case is meaningless unless there is a measurement at some time of whether the claimed benefits have been achieved. The approach to confirming benefit achievement is to:

- Identify the benefits.
- Identify objective measures of benefit achievement.
- Assemble measurements of the current situation against which the improvements will be compared.
- Decide how, when and by whom benefits will be measured.

The Senior User(s) specifies the benefits and must demonstrate to corporate or programme management that the forecast benefits that formed the basis of project approval are in fact realized. This may involve a commitment beyond the life of the project as it is likely that many benefits will not be realized until after the project has closed.

This is a problem, as once the project closes the 'temporary organization' is disbanded. So who will carry out any measurement activities and does the project need to set aside money to pay for the measurement exercise?

PRINCE2 overcomes this dilemma by creating a Benefits Review Plan. This takes the claimed benefits in the Business Case and defines the timing, measuring methods and responsibilities of one or more benefit reviews. (Remember, some benefits may be achieved within the lifecycle of the project.)

The Benefits Review Plan is first created by the Project Manager in the initiation stage and is submitted to the Project Board for approval as part of seeking project authorization. The Benefits Review Plan is updated towards the end of each stage with any benefits achieved and a revised plan is created for any remaining reviews whether within or beyond the life of the project.

The Executive is normally responsible for ensuring that benefits reviews are planned, but for projects in a programme environment, the project's Benefits Review Plan will be produced and executed by the programme. For projects that are not part of a programme, the responsibility for benefits reviews will transfer from the Executive to corporate management as the project closes (as the reviews will need to be funded and resourced).

As the Benefits Review Plan may be managed by the project, corporate or programme management, PRINCE2 recommends that it is kept separate from the Project and Stage Plans.

The post-project benefits review(s) will involve corporate or programme management asking the Senior User(s) to provide evidence of the benefits gained in comparison to those benefits promised when justifying the cost and risk of the project when it was authorized. The post-project benefits review(s) will also review the performance of the project's products in operational use and identify if there have been any side-effects (beneficial or adverse) that may provide useful lessons for other projects.

10.7 LINKS

A basic Business Case should appear in the project mandate or be developed as part of preparing the Project Brief.

There is a major link with the initiation stage, in which the Project Manager should finalize the Business Case before the Project Board decides whether or not the project should be undertaken.

The Business Case should be revised at the end of each stage as part of *Managing a Stage Boundary* (also in the event of raising an Exception Plan). This feeds into the end-stage assessment, which is the review by the Project Board in *Authorize a Stage or Exception Plan*, as part of its decision on whether or not to continue with the project.

The impact on the Business Case is assessed for each major issue as part of the activity *Capture and Examine Issues and Risks*.

Achievement of the Business Case is finally judged when implementing the Benefits Review Plan after project closure.

The implications of risk management should be linked to the Business Case.

10.8 IF IT IS A LARGE PROJECT

The Business Case is likely to take some time to prepare. There should be at least the outline of a Business Case in the project mandate that triggered the project. Creating the full Business Case is likely to take some time in a large project, so do not rush through initiation by customers who are yelling 'Just get on with it!' They are the ones who will be asking 'Is it worth it?' half way through the project or at the end.

10.9 IF IT IS A SMALL PROJECT

Do not ignore the philosophy that there should be business justification for every project. A lot of small projects undertaken without business justification can waste as much as one large project. It may be satisfactory to carry out a short, informal Business Case appraisal, but the Executive should still be convinced that a genuine Business Case exists.

Chapter 11

Organization

11.1 PHILOSOPHY

The organization theme supports the principle of defined roles and responsibilities.

PRINCE2 recognizes that three interests must always be represented in the decision-making body of a project. The anagram of this is B/U/S (Figure 11.1):

- The business;
- The user;
- The supplier.

The business interest covers the funding of the project and the benefits from the outcome. The user interest represents those who will use, maintain or will be affected by the final product(s). The supplier interest covers the resources that will build the products.

The organization for a PRINCE2 project is also based on a customer/supplier relationship. The customer is the person or group who

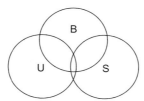

FIGURE 11.1   Business, user and supplier interests.

wants the end product, specifies what it should be and, usually, pays for the development of that product. The supplier is the one who provides the resources to build or procure the end product.

This is true even if the customer and the supplier work for the same company. If this is the case they may still report to different lines of management, have different budgets and therefore have a different view of the finances of the project. The customer will be asking, 'Will the end product save me money or bring in a profit?'. The supplier will be asking if the provision of appropriate resources will earn a profit.

Establishing an effective organizational structure for the project is crucial to its success. Every project needs direction, management, control and communication. Before you start any project, you should establish what the project organization is to be. You need to ask the questions *even if it is a very small project*. Answers to these questions will separate the real decision-makers from those who have opinions, identify responsibilities and accountability, and establish a structure for communication. Examples of the questions to ask are:

- Who is providing the funds?
- Who has the authority to say what is needed?
- Who is providing the development resources?
- Who will manage the project on a day-to-day basis?
- How many different sets of specialist skills are needed?
- Who will establish and maintain the required standards?
- Who will safeguard the developed products?
- Who will know where all the documents are?
- What are the limits to the Project Manager's authority and who sets those limits?

11.2 OVERVIEW

To fulfill the philosophy, PRINCE2 has a project management team structure (Figure 11.2).

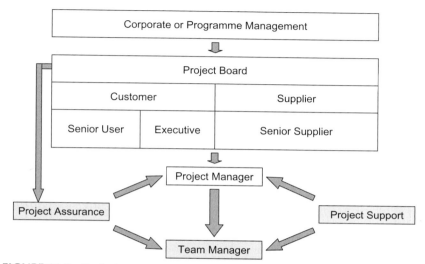

FIGURE 11.2   Project management team structure.

It is good to have a generic project management structure that can be tailored to any project. Without knowing anything about a project's size or complexity we can understand the same organizational terms and, by fitting names to these, understand quickly who does what. But with one structure for all sizes of project, it is important that it is flexible; a structure that can be suitable for large as well as small projects. The only way in which we can do this is to talk about *roles* that need to be filled, rather than jobs that need to be allocated on a one-to-one basis to individuals. In order to be flexible and meet the needs of different environments and different project sizes, the PRINCE2 structure defines roles that might be allocated to one person, shared with others or combined according to a project's needs. Examples are given later in the chapter.

Corporate or programme management hand the decision-making for a project to the Project Board. The Project Board members are busy in their own right and do not have the time to look after the project on a day-to-day basis. They delegate this to the Project Manager, reserving to themselves the key stop/go decisions. If they are too busy or do not have the current expertise, they can appoint someone to a Project Assurance role to monitor an aspect of the project on their behalf. A typical example here would be the participation of a company's quality assurance function on behalf of the Senior User or the Senior Supplier. (Note: They would take a Project Assurance role as far as PRINCE2 is concerned, not quality assurance.) Another example of the Project Assurance role would be a role for Internal Audit.

Depending on the project environment or the Project Manager's expertise, he or she might need some support. This might be purely administrative, such jobs as filing, travel planning or note taking, but might also include specialist jobs such as configuration management or expertise in the planning and control software tool that is to be used on the project.

11.3 PROJECT BOARD

11.3.1 General

The Project Board is appointed by corporate or programme management to provide overall direction and management of the project. The Project Board is accountable for the success of the project, and has responsibility and authority for the project within the limits set by corporate/programme management.

The Project Board is the project's 'voice' to the outside world and is responsible for any publicity or other dissemination of information about the project.

11.3.2 Specific Responsibilities

The Project Board approves all major plans and authorizes any major deviation from agreed Stage Plans. It is the authority that signs off the completion of each stage as well as authorizes the start of the next stage. It ensures that required resources are committed and arbitrates on any conflicts within the project or negotiates a solution to any problems between the project and external bodies.

In addition, the Project Board approves the appointment and responsibilities of the Project Manager and any delegation of its Project Assurance responsibilities.

The Project Board is ultimately responsible for Project Assurance, ensuring that it remains on course to deliver the desired outcome of the required quality to meet the Business Case defined in the project contract. According to the size, complexity and risk of the project, the Project Board may decide to delegate some of the Project Assurance responsibility. Later in this chapter Project Assurance is defined in more detail.

Responsibilities of specific members of the Project Board are described below.

11.4 EXECUTIVE

11.4.1 General

The Executive is ultimately responsible for the project, supported by the Senior User and the Senior Supplier. The Executive has to ensure that the project offers value for money, ensuring a cost-conscious approach to the project, balancing the demands of business, user and supplier.

Throughout the project the Executive 'owns' the Business Case.

The Executive is responsible for overall business assurance of the project, i.e. it reflects the company's strategy, remains on target to deliver products that will achieve the expected business benefits, and will complete within its agreed tolerances for budget and schedule.

11.5 SENIOR USER

11.5.1 General

The Senior User is responsible for the specification of the needs of all those who will use the final product(s), user liaison with the project team and for monitoring that the solution will meet those needs within the constraints of the Business Case.

The Senior User(s) represents the interests of all those who will use the final product(s) of the project, those for whom the product will achieve an objective or those who will use the product to deliver benefits. The Senior User role commits any required user resources and monitors products against requirements. This role may require more than one person to cover all user interests. For the sake of effectiveness the role should not be split among too many people.

11.6 SENIOR SUPPLIER

11.6.1 General

The role represents the interests of those designing, developing, facilitating, procuring and implementing the project products. The Senior Supplier is responsible for the quality of all products supplied by the suppliers. The role must have the authority to commit or acquire supplier resources required.

In more complex projects more than one person may be required to represent the suppliers.

11.7 PROJECT MANAGER

11.7.1 General

The Project Manager has the authority to run the project on a day-to-day basis on behalf of the Project Board within the constraints laid down by the board. In a customer/supplier environment the Project Manager will normally come from the customer organization.

The Project Manager's prime responsibility is to ensure that the project produces the required products, according to the required standard of quality and within the specified constraints of time and cost. The Project Manager is also responsible for the project producing a result that is capable of achieving the benefits defined in the Business Case.

11.8 TEAM MANAGER

11.8.1 General

This role leads a team to implement a Work Package. The allocation of this role to one or more people is optional. Where the project does not warrant the use of a Team Manager, the Project Manager takes the role.

The Project Manager may find that it is beneficial to delegate the authority and responsibility for planning the creation of certain products and managing a team of technicians to produce those products. There are many reasons why it may be decided to employ this role:

- Size of the project;
- The particular specialist skills or knowledge needed for certain products;
- Geographical location of some team members;
- Preferences of the Project Board.

The Team Manager's prime responsibility is to ensure production of those products defined by the Project Manager to an appropriate quality as defined in the Product Descriptions, in a timescale and at a cost acceptable to the Project Board. The Team Manager reports to and takes direction from the Project Manager.

The use of this role should be discussed by the Project Manager with the Project Board and, if the role is required, planned at the outset of the project. This is discussed in the *Starting up a Project* (SU) and *Initiating a Project* (IP) processes.

11.9 PROJECT ASSURANCE

11.9.1 General

The Project Board members do not work full-time on the project; therefore they place a great deal of reliance on the Project Manager.

Although they receive regular reports from the Project Manager, there may always be questions at the back of their minds:

- Are things really going as well as we are being told?
- Are any problems being hidden from us?
- Is the solution going to be what we want?
- Are we suddenly going to find that the project is over-budget or late?

All of these points mean that there is a need in the project management team for monitoring all aspects of the project's performance and products independent of the Project Manager. This is the Project Assurance function.

These Project Assurance functions are part of the role of each Project Board member. According to the needs and desires of the Project Board, any of these Project Assurance responsibilities can be delegated, as long as the recipients are independent of the Project Manager and the rest of the project management team. Any appointed Project Assurance jobs assure the project on behalf of one or more members of the Project Board.

Note that Project Assurance roles are only delegated. The Project Board member retains accountability. Any delegation should be documented.

It is not mandatory that all Project Assurance roles be delegated. Each of the Project Assurance roles delegated may be assigned to one individual or shared. Each Project Board member decides when his/her Project Assurance role needs to be delegated. It may be for the entire project or for only a part of it. The person or persons filling a Project Assurance role may be changed during the project at the request of the Project Board member. Any use of Project Assurance roles should be planned in the initiation stage. There is no stipulation on how many Project Assurance roles there must be.

Project Assurance has to be independent of the Project Manager; therefore the Project Board cannot delegate any of its Project Assurance responsibilities to the Project Manager.

11.9.2 Specific

- Maintenance of thorough liaison throughout the project between the supplier and the customer.
- The user needs and expectations are being met or managed.
- Risks are being controlled.
- Adherence to the Business Case.
- Constant reassessment of the value-for-money solution.
- Ensuring a fit with the overall programme or company strategy.
- The right people are involved in writing Product Descriptions.
- The right people are planned for involvement in quality checking at the correct points in the product's development.
- Staff are properly trained in the quality checking procedures.
- The quality review/quality checking procedures are being correctly followed.
- The quality checking follow-up actions are dealt with correctly.
- An acceptable solution is being developed.
- The project remains viable.
- The scope of the project is not 'creeping upwards' unnoticed.
- Focus on the business need is maintained.
- Internal and external communications are working.
- The applicable standards are being used.
- Any legislative constraints are being observed.
- The needs of business interests (e.g. security) are being observed.
- Adherence to quality assurance standards.

11.10 PROJECT SUPPORT

11.10.1 General

The provision of any Project Support on a formal basis is optional. It is driven by the needs of the individual project and Project Manager. Project Support could be in the form of advice on project management tools and administrative services, such as filing, the collection of actual data, to one or more related projects. Where set up as an official body, Project Support can act as a repository for lessons learned, and a central source of expertise in specialist support tools.

One support function that must be considered is that of configuration management. Depending on the project size and environment, there may be a need to formalize this, and it quickly becomes a task with which the Project Manager cannot cope without support. See the chapter on Configuration Management for details of the work.

Chapter 12

Plans

12.1 OVERVIEW

It is impossible to control a project without a plan. Without a plan you do not know whether you are ahead of the game, on target or way behind schedule. A plan gives you:

- Targets;
- The products needed to meet the targets;
- The work needed to create the products;
- The resources and skills needed to do the work;
- Any equipment needed by the resources;
- The sequence in which the products are required;
- The time it will take to create each product;
- A basis for work allocation;
- The ability to see product development matched with the resources across a timeframe;
- A view on whether the targets are achievable;
- A view of any risks inherent in the resources used and timing of the plan;
- A communication device for all those involved in the plan.

This chapter looks at the question of planning for a project.

12.2 HIERARCHY OF PLANS

12.2.1 Project Plan

The Project Plan is created at the start of the project. The original Project Plan is a part of the Project Initiation Documentation. In my opinion, the Project Plan is a mandatory plan in PRINCE2 (Figure 12.1). The 2009 version of the manual does not say this. In fact it says nothing about the Project Plan. In my experience the Project Plan is mandatory and the failure to mention this is an omission in the manual.

The Project Board does not want to know about every detailed activity in the project. It requires a high-level view. This allows the Project Board to know:

- How long the project will take;
- What the major deliverables or products will be;
- Roughly when these will be delivered;
- What people and other resources will have to be committed in order to meet the plan;
- How control will be exerted;
- How quality will be maintained;
- What risks exist in the approach taken.

The Project Board will control the project using the Project Plan as a yardstick of progress.

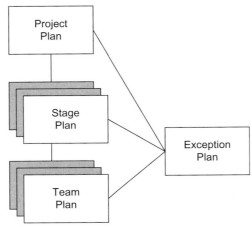

FIGURE 12.1   The PRINCE2 hierarchy of plans.

The Project Plan provides the Business Case with the costs and timescale.

12.2.2 Stage Plan

Stage Plans are also mandatory. Unless a project is very small, it will be easier to plan in detail one stage at a time. Another part of the philosophy that makes stage planning easier is that a stage is planned shortly before it is due to start, so you have the latest information on actual progress so far available to you.

Having specified the stages and major products in the Project Plan, each stage is then planned in a greater level of detail. This is done just before the end of the previous stage.

The procedure at stage planning time involves taking those major products in the Project Plan that are to be created during that stage, and breaking these down to further levels of detail until you have reached a level where you can estimate the time and resources required with reasonable accuracy.

12.2.3 Team Plan

Team Plans are optional. Their use is dictated by the size, complexity and risks associated with the project.

Team Plans are the lowest level of detail and should specify activities down to the level of a handful of days, say 10 at most.

Team Plans will be needed when internal or external teams are to do portions of the work. Part of the Project Manager's job is to cross-relate these plans to the Project and Stage Plans. If the Team Plan is produced by an external supplier, the Project Manager may not be able to insist that the plan is produced to PRINCE2 standards.

12.2.4 Exception Plan

Finally, there is the Exception Plan. This is produced when a plan is predicted to exceed the tolerances agreed upon between the planner and the next higher level of authority. The Exception Plan takes over from the plan it is replacing and has the same format.

If a Stage Plan is forecast to deviate, the Project Board may ask the Project Manager for an Exception Plan to replace the remainder of the current Stage Plan. If the Project Plan threatens to fall outside its tolerances, corporate or programme management would decide whether to ask for an Exception Plan to replace the remainder of the Project Plan.

If a Team Plan is forecast to deviate beyond tolerances, the Project Manager may modify the Work Package as long as it is within stage tolerances. If this cannot be done within stage tolerances, then the stage is in exception and must follow the process described above. The manual suggests that an Exception Plan is not needed to replace a Team Plan, and that the recovery can be made simply by the Project Manager changing the Work Package or issuing a new one. This still leaves the question of what the Team Manager uses to control the team's work. In my opinion, this must be a Team Plan.

12.3 THE PRINCE2 APPROACH TO PLANNING

The PRINCE2 planning philosophy is that all plans should start by identifying the products that will be produced by or are required for that plan (Figure 12.2).

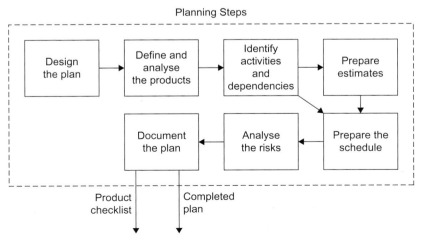

FIGURE 12.2   The planning steps.

12.3.1 Design a Plan

- Decides how many levels of plan are needed by the project;
- Identifies any planning tools to be used;
- Identifies the method(s) of estimating to be used.

This activity is carried out onsly once per project, before the first plan is created. It defines the standards to be used in all future plans. The result should be a consistent set of plans.

How?

- Decide what levels of plan are needed for the project, i.e. Project Plan, Stage Plans, Team Plans.
- Ascertain if the organisation or programme uses a particular planning tool as standard.
- Identify the planning tool to be used in the initial Project Plan, part of the Project Initiation Documentation.
- Identify what estimating method(s) are available and suitable for the project.
- Ensure that the estimating method(s) chosen contain allowances for issue analysis, telephone calls, ad hoc meetings, learning curves, experience, etc.
- Discuss with the Project Board the format in which plans should be presented.
- Discuss with the Project Board whether there should be a Change Budget set aside.
- Discuss with the Project Board whether there should be a separate allowance for any anticipated Contingency Plans.

12.3.2 Define and Analyse Products

PRINCE2 uses a Product-based Planning technique to define and analyse a plan's products. In general terms this technique:

- Identifies the products whose delivery has to be planned;
- Describes each of the products in terms of purpose, composition and quality criteria and ensures that these descriptions are agreed upon by all concerned;

- Identifies the sequence of delivering the products and the dependencies between them.

By defining the products and their quality requirements, everyone can see and understand the required plan result. It means that who-ever has to deliver a product knows in advance what its purpose is, to what quality it has to be built and what interfaces there are with other products.

The technique is described with examples in Section 12.4.

12.3.3 Identify Activities and Dependencies

This step:

- Identifies all activities necessary to deliver the products;
- Defines the dependencies between the activities [based on the dependencies shown in the Product Flow Diagram (PFD)].

For Stage and Team Plans the Product Flow Diagram may still be at too high a level for the purposes of estimation and control. This optional activity allows a further breakdown, based on the Product Flow Diagram, until each activity will last only a handful of days.

How?
- Consider if a product in the Product Flow Diagram is too big to estimate or would need such a large effort that it would be dif-ficult to control against that estimate.
- When a product is too big, break it down into the activities needed to produce it. This should continue down to the level where an activity is less than 10 days effort, ideally no more than five days.
- When a product has been broken down into several activities, put the activities into their correct sequence.
- Review the dependencies between products and refine them to give dependencies between the new activities. For example, where Product Flow Diagram dependencies went from the end of one product to the start of the next, is there now an opportunity

to overlap or start some activities on a product before all the activities on its preceding product have been done?

12.3.4 Prepare Estimates

This step:

- Identifies the types of resources needed for the plan;
- Estimates the effort for each activity/product.

The objective is to identify the resources and effort required to complete each activity or product.

How?

- Examine each activity/product and identify what resource types it requires. Apart from human resources there may be other resources needed, such as equipment. With human resources, consider and document what level of skill you are basing the estimate on.
- Judge what level of efficiency you will base your estimates on, what allowance for non-project time you will need to use.
- Estimate the effort needed for each activity/product.
- Understand whether that is an estimate of uninterrupted work, to which the allowances must be added, or whether the estimate already includes allowances.
- Document any assumptions you have made, e.g. the use of specific named resources, levels of skill and experience, the availability of user resources when you need them. Check the assumptions with those who have such knowledge, such as the Senior Supplier and Senior User.

12.3.5 Prepare the Schedule

This step:

- Matches resources to activities/products;
- Schedules work according to sequence and dependencies;
- Adjusts the schedule to avoid people being over- or under-utilized;
- Negotiates a solution with the Project Board for problems such as too few resources, too many resources or inability to meet fixed target dates;

- Calculates the cost of the resources used in the plan.

A plan can only show whether it can meet its targets when the activities are put together in a schedule against a timeframe, showing when activities will be done and by what resources.

How?

- Draw a planning network.
- Assess resource availability. This should include dates of availability as well as what the scale of that availability is. Any known information on holidays and training courses should be gathered.
- Allocate activities to resources and produce a draft schedule.
- Revise the draft to remove as many peaks and troughs in resource usage as possible.
- Add in management and quality activities or products (Stage and Team Plans only).
- Add in, if appropriate, any milestones where comparison of actual progress against the plan will show if work is proceeding as expected. An example of a milestone would be a trigger for payment to a supplier.
- Calculate resource utilisation and costs.

12.3.6 Analyse the Risks

This step:

- Checks the draft plan for any risks.

You should not commit to a plan without considering what risks are involved and what impact the plan might have on risks already known.

How?

- Look for any external dependencies. These always represent one or more risks. They might not arrive on time. They might be of poor quality or be wrong in some other way.

- Look for any assumptions you have made in the plan, e.g. the resources available to you. Each assumption is a risk.
- Look at each resource in the plan. Is there a risk involved? For example, that a new resource does not perform at the expected level, or a resource's availability is not achieved.
- Are the tools or technology unproven?
- Take the appropriate risk actions. Where appropriate, revise the plan. Make sure that any new or modified risks are shown in the Risk Register.

12.3.7 Document the Plan

This step adds text to explain the plan.

A plan should not be simply a diagram, a Gantt chart or a tabular list of products and target dates. Plans should have a narrative section.

Suggested headings for the narrative are:

- Plan description;
- Quality plan;
- Plan assumptions;
- Plan prerequisites;
- External dependencies;
- Risks;
- Tolerance;
- Reporting.

How?
- Agree upon tolerance levels for the plan.
- Document what the plan covers, the approach to the work and the checking of its quality.
- Document any assumptions you have made.
- Add the planning dates to the Product Checklist (if used).
- Publish the plan.

12.4 PRODUCT-BASED PLANNING

12.4.1 The Benefits of Product-Based Planning

PRINCE2 recommends Product-based Planning. There are two reasons for this. Firstly, a project delivers products, not activities, so why begin at a lower level? The second reason is about quality. We can measure the quality of a product. The quality of an activity can only be measured by the quality of its outcome (the product). Other benefits include:

- A consistent and unambiguous way of describing each product;
- A discipline to think of the purpose(s) of each product before creating it;
- A discipline to think of the quality required by a product before creating it;
- A visual way of defining the scope of a plan;
- The involvement of users in defining the products;
- The identification of products required by the project that either already exist or are to be created by projects outside the Project Manager's control (called external products).

Product-based Planning has four parts (Figure 12.3):

- Write the Project Product Description.
- Create the Product Breakdown Structure.
- Write the Product Description.
- Create the Product Flow Diagram.

12.4.2 Write the Project Product Description

This is a summary of the project's final product. It defines what the project must deliver in order to be accepted by the customer. It is officially the responsibility of the Senior User, but usually the Project Manager writes it in consultation with the Senior User and the Executive. A description of its contents can be found in Appendix A.

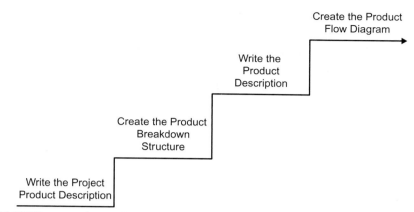

FIGURE 12.3 The product-based planning steps.

12.4.3 Create the Product Breakdown Structure

A Product Breakdown Structure is a hierarchy of the products (or ideas about a group of products) that the plan requires to produce. At the top of the hierarchy is the final end product, e.g. a computer system, a new yacht, a department relocated to a new building. This is then broken down into its major constituents at the next level. Each constituent is then broken down into its parts, and this theme continues until the planner has reached the level of detail required for the plan.

12.4.4 Write the Product Description

For each significant product, at all levels of the Product Breakdown Structure, a description is produced. Its creation forces the planner to consider if sufficient information is known about the product in order to plan its production. It is also the first time that the quality of an individual product is considered.

The purposes of writing a Product Description are, therefore, to provide a guide:

* To the planner in how much effort will be required to create the product;

- To the author of the product on what is required;
- Against which the finished product can be measured.

These descriptions are a vital checklist to be used when building and at a quality check of the related products.

The description should contain:

- The purpose of the product;
- The products from which it is derived;
- The composition of the product;
- Any standards for format and presentation;
- The quality criteria to be applied to the product;
- The quality verification method to be used.

The Product Description is given to both the product's creator and those who will verify its quality.

12.4.5 Create the Product Flow Diagram

The Product Flow Diagram is a diagram showing the sequence in which the products have to be produced and the dependencies between them. The products are those shown in the Product Breakdown Structure and care should be taken to ensure that the same names are used for products in the two diagrams.

Not all 'products' in a Product Breakdown Structure need to be transferred to the Product Flow Diagram. Some of them may not be products in their own right but thoughts for a series of products that will be needed. For example, if the project is to create a training manual, one 'product' may be 'translations'. You are not going to produce a product called 'translations', but it will trigger you to think of real products like translations into German, French, etc. 'Translations' would not be transferred to the Product Flow Diagram. So, only REAL products in the Product Breakdown Structure are transferred to the Product Flow Diagram. The sample at the end of this section shows examples of such 'non-products'.

A Product Flow Diagram normally needs only three symbols; a rectangle to contain products developed within the plan, an ellipse for external products and an arrow to show the dependencies.

12.4.6 External Products

There are times when you may wish to show that the plan is dependent on a product that already exists or over whose delivery you have no control. For example, you might have to create a product 'packaged disks'. Before you can create this product you have to receive the plastic disk box from the stock of an external supplier. To show that the development of the plastic disk box is outside your control you would use a different symbol. PRINCE2 uses an ellipse. The Product Flow Diagram for this example would be:

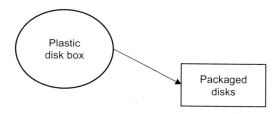

12.4.7 Product States

One subject that causes debate is whether a product that passes through several states should be shown as one product or as a product for each state. For example, if in relocating a factory you have 'dismantled machinery', 'transported machinery' and 'reassembled machinery', there may be good reasons for treating these as three products; there would be different purposes, quality criteria and quality checks, and different teams may be used for each state. On the other hand, a document will have several states, such as draft, reviewed, proof-read and published. Do you really need to write a Product Description for each of these states? It can usually be done by one Product Description with quality criteria for each of these 'states'.

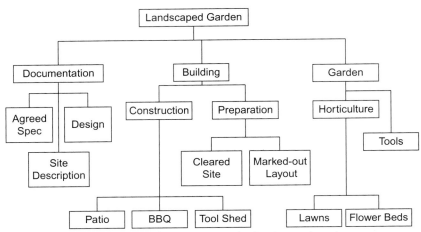

FIGURE 12.4   Product Breakdown Structure for landscaped garden.

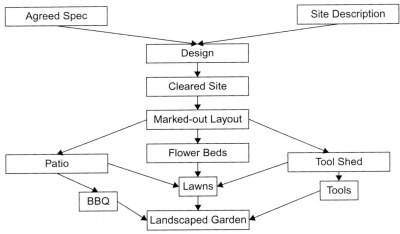

FIGURE 12.5   Product Flow Diagram for landscaped garden.

12.4.8 Sample

Let us take an example of a project whose objective is to design and construct a garden. For the sake of an example we shall keep this simple (Figures 12.4 and 12.5).

Chapter 13

Progress

13.1 INTRODUCTION

Three of the PRINCE2 Principles are supported by the Progress theme. These are:

- Management by stages;
- Management by exception;
- Continued business justification.

The purpose of the Progress theme is to define the points in a project at which control should be exercised, and the PRINCE2 responsibilities, documentation and procedures for monitoring progress at these points, and comparing actual progress against plans.

13.2 PROJECT BOARD CONTROLS

As defined in the Directing a Project process, the Project Board has five control points.

13.2.1 Authorize Initiation

This is where the Project Board decides if the Project Brief and outline Business Case can sufficiently justify the initiation stage.

13.2.2 Authorize a Project

This is where the Project Board decides if there is agreement on:

- What the project is to achieve?
- Why it is being undertaken?
- Who is to be involved and in what role?
- How and when the required products will be delivered?

This information is documented in the Project Initiation Documentation, which is then 'frozen' and used by the Project Board as a benchmark throughout the project and at the end to check the performance and deliveries of the project.

13.2.3 Authorize a Stage

A stage is a collection of activities and deliverables whose delivery is managed as a unit. As such, it is a subset of the project, and in PRINCE2 terms it is the element of work that the Project Manager is managing on behalf of the Project Board at any one time.

The reasons for breaking projects into management stages are to give the Project Board opportunities for conscious decision-making as to whether to continue with the project, based upon:

- A formal analysis of how the project is performing, based on information about results of the current stage;
- An assessment of the next Stage Plan;
- A check on what impact the next Stage Plan will have on the overall Project Plan;
- A check to confirm that the business justification for the project is still valid;
- Confirmation that the risks facing the project are manageable.

At the end of each stage, the Project Board can stop the project if it determines that the project is no longer viable. For example, the organisation's business needs may have changed to the point that the project is no longer cost-effective. A project may also be cancelled if the estimated cost to complete the project exceeds the available funds.

Unless the project is broken into stages to provide suitable points at which to make the decisions, the Project Board cannot be fully in control of the project and its resources.

Number of Stages

A PRINCE2 project must have at least two stages: initiation and the rest of the project. Initiation is always the first stage. It prepares the Project Initiation Document and submits it to the Project Board to ask for the project to be authorized.

The question of how may stages to break a project into depends on balancing a number of factors:

- How far ahead in the project is it sensible to plan?
- Which are the key decision points in the project?
- How risky is the project?
- Too many short stages increase the administration overhead, too few lengthy stages reduce the level of Project Board control.

13.2.4 Give Ad Hoc Direction

This Project Board activity contains three controls.

Highlight Reports

At a frequency defined by the Project Board in the Project Initiation Documentation, the Project Manager sends a Highlight Report to the Project Board to review progress and achievements in the current stage.

Exception Reports

If the Project Manager can forecast that the plan will end outside its tolerance margins, an Exception Report must be sent immediately to the Project Board detailing the problem, the options and a recommendation.

Management by Exception

Tolerance is the permissible deviation from a plan without having to refer the matter to the next higher level of authority.

There are six elements of tolerance:

- Time;
- Cost;
- Quality;
- Scope;
- Risk;
- Benefit.

No project has ever gone 100% according to the plan. There will be good days and bad days, good weeks and bad weeks. If the Project Board is going to 'manage by exception', it does not want the Project Manager running to it, saying, 'I've spent a dollar more than I should today' or 'I've fallen an hour behind schedule this week'. But equally the Project Board does not want the project to over-spend by a $million or slip two months behind schedule without being warned. So where is the dividing line? What size of deviation from the plan is OK without going back to the board for a decision? These margins are the tolerances.

The second philosophical point about tolerances is that we do not wait for tolerances to be exceeded; we forecast this, so that the next higher level of authority has time to react and possibly prevent or reduce the deviation or exception.

Project tolerances should be part of the project mandate handed down by corporate/programme management. If they are not there, it is the Executive's job to find out from corporate/programme management what they are.

The Project Board sets stage tolerances for the Project Manager within the overall project tolerances that it has received. The portion allocated to a stage should depend on the risk content of the work, the extent of the unknowns, such as technologies never used before, resources of unknown ability and tasks never attempted before.

The Project Manager negotiates appropriate tolerances for each Work Package with the Team Manager. Again these will be sub-tolerances within the stage tolerances set for the Project Manager.

As long as the plan's actual progress is within the tolerance margins, all is well. As soon as it can be *forecast* that progress will deviate outside the tolerance margins, the next higher level of authority needs to be advised.

13.2.5 Authorize Project Closure

The final control point for the Project Board is to confirm that the project has done everything it was told to, all completed products have been handed over and resources may now be released.

13.3 PROJECT MANAGER CONTROLS

13.3.1 Risk Register

Risks are examined:

- Before starting the project (*Starting up a Project* and authorizing initiation);
- Before commencing a new stage (*Managing a Stage Boundary* and authorizing a project);
- As part of the analysis of any major change (*Capture and Examine Issues and Risks*);
- Before confirming project closure (*Closing a Project* and authorizing project closure).

13.3.2 Issue Register

Having approved the objectives and products required in the project initiation, it is only right that the Project Board should have to approve any changes to them. Once requested changes have been estimated for the effort and cost of doing them, the customer has to decide on their priority, whether they should be done and whether the money to do them can be found. As for all the other decisions, it needs an assessment of the impact on the Project Plan, the Business Case and the risk situation.

13.3.3 Work Packages   ⌣ ⊂ϟ

A Work Package is an agreement between the Project Manager and a Team Manager to undertake a piece of work. It describes the work, agreed dates, standards to be used, quality and reporting require-ments. No work can start without the Project Manager's approval via a Work Package, so it is a powerful schedule, cost and quality control for the Project Manager.

13.3.4 Checkpoint Reports

This is a report from a Team Manager to the Project Manager. It is sent at a frequency agreed upon in the Work Package.

The information gathered in Checkpoint Reports is recorded for the Project Manager and forms the basis of the Highlight Report.

13.3.5 Quality Register

The Quality Register records every planned quality check, plus details of when it actually happened, who participated and what the results were. It provides the Project Manager with an overview of what is happening with regard to quality. Team Managers provide details of the actual quality checks and Project Support updates the Quality Register.

13.4 EVENT-DRIVEN AND TIME-DRIVEN CONTROLS

Some PRINCE2 controls are event-driven, others are time-driven. Below is a table showing which controls are time-driven and which are event-driven.

TABLE 13.1

	Event-driven	Time-driven
Project Initiation	√	
Stages	√	
Management by Exception	√	
End Stage Assessment	√	
Highlight Report		√
Exception Report	√	
Work Package	√	
Checkpoint Report		√
Risk Register	√	
Quality Register	√	
Issue Register	√	

Chapter 14

Quality

14.1 PHILOSOPHY

The Quality theme defines the PRINCE2 approach to ensuring that the project will create and verify products that are fit for purpose.

The Quality theme supports the Principles of focus on products and defined roles and responsibilities.

Any thoughts or actions about quality in a project must start by finding out what the customer's quality expectations are. It is dangerous to assume that the customer will always want a superb quality product that will last forever. Have a look at the products in your local cut-price store and you will see what different levels of quality criteria there are.

14.2 QUALITY DEFINITION

PRINCE2 uses the ISO definition of quality:

'The totality of features and inherent or assigned characteristics of a product, person, process, service and/or system that bear on its ability to show that it meets expectations or satisfies stated needs, requirements or specification'.

14.3 THE QUALITY PATH

Part of the PRINCE2 quality philosophy is that quality is built into every phase of a product's specification and development and is not left to a check before final delivery.

TABLE 14.1

STEP	PRODUCT	PROCESS/ TECHNIQUE/THEME
Ascertain the customer's quality expectations	Project mandate or Project Brief	Starting Up a Project (SU)
Document the customer's quality expectations and acceptance criteria	Project Product Description	Starting Up a Project (SU)
Write a Quality Management Strategy	Project Initiation Documentation	Initiating a Project
Write a Stage Quality Plan	Stage Plan	Managing a Stage Boundary
Record planned quality activities	Quality Register	Managing a Stage Boundary
Define an individual product's quality criteria	Product Description	Product-based Planning
Explain the techniques, interfaces, constraints and configuration management requirements for each piece of work	Work Package	Controlling a Stage
Report back on the quality work performed	Quality Register	Managing Product Delivery
Check that quality work is being done correctly	Quality Register	Controlling a Stage
Control changes	Issue Register	Change
Keep track of changes to products	Configuration Item Records	Configuration Management

14.3.1 Customer's Quality Expectations

The customer's quality expectations should be made clear in the project mandate at the very outset of the project. If not sufficiently clear, the Project Manager should clarify the expectations when preparing the Project Product Description [during *Starting up a Project* (SU)]. The customer's quality expectations are often expressed in terms that are too broad to be measurable.

14.3.2 Acceptance Criteria

These turn the customer's quality expectations into measurable terms. 'Of good quality' may sound fine as an expectation, but how can it be measured?

A project's acceptance criteria are a set of measurable attributes of the final product(s). The PRINCE2 concept is that the acceptance criteria must be met before the user accepts the final product. However, some acceptance criteria cannot be measured until the final product has been operational for some time. Such criteria must be added to the Benefits Review Plan.

Acceptance criteria may be split into 'time zones'. Some must be fully met before the project can be closed, but for others, such as performance, there may be a series of improving targets that must be met after periods of operational use.

Acceptance criteria should also be prioritized in case there comes a time when one criterion can only be fully met at the expense of another one. For example, delivery on time vs. having a product that is 100% complete.

Expectations of performance, reliability, flexibility, maintainability and capability can all be expressed in measurable terms.

14.4 THE PROJECT PRODUCT DESCRIPTION

This specialized form of a Product Description is created during *Starting Up a Project* and may be refined during initiation. It is used in *Closing a Project* to check that the acceptance criteria have been met. It includes:

• The purpose of the final product;
• The set of major products of which it consists;

- The customer's quality expectations;
- Acceptance criteria;
- Project level quality tolerances.

14.5 THE QUALITY MANAGEMENT STRATEGY

The next step is to decide how the project is going to meet the customer's quality expectations for the product. This is documented in a Quality Management Strategy, created in the *Initiating a Project* process.

Other inputs to this should be the standards to be used to guide the development of the product and test its ability to meet the quality expectations. The supplier should have standards, but the customer may also have standards that he/she insists on being used. Such standards have to be compared against the expectations to see which are to be used. There may be gaps where extra standards have to be obtained or created. The customer has the last say in what standards will be used to check the products. There may also be regulatory standards to be met.

14.5.1 PRINCE2 and A Company's Quality Management System

There may be confusion here between two uses of the initials QMS. In PRINCE2 this is the Quality Management Strategy, described in this section. The other use is for a company's Quality Management System, a document covering all the standards that a company needs for its functions, and not only project management. PRINCE2 may form part of a company's Quality Management System where project management standards are defined.

14.5.2 Quality Management Strategy Responsibilities

The Quality Management Strategy identifies the standards to be used and the main quality responsibilities. The latter may be a reference to a quality assurance function (belonging to either the customer or the supplier or both). There is a cross-reference here to the Project Board roles. These roles contain Project Assurance responsibilities, some of them affecting quality. If these have been delegated, there must be a match with the responsibilities defined in the Quality Management Strategy.

14.6 PROJECT ASSURANCE VS. QUALITY ASSURANCE

There is often confusion between these two terms.

Project Assurance refers to the Project Board's accountability for assuring that the project is conducted properly in all respects. This is, therefore, a responsibility within the project organization.

Quality assurance is the function within a company that establishes and maintains the Quality Management System for the whole company. Quality assurance activities are therefore outside the scope of PRINCE2 and the responsibility of corporate or programme management.

It is sensible to arrange for quality assurance independent of the project management team. Quality assurance provides a check that the project's direction and management are adequate for the nature of the project and that it complies with relevant corporate or programme management standards and policies.

14.7 QUALITY REGISTER

This is created in the *Initiating a Project* process. It is a record of all planned quality activities and the results of those activities. A suggested structure is shown in Appendix A.

The Quality Register is updated during *Managing a Stage Boundary* when planning the next stage. Details of planned checks are added. This should include the planned date of the check plus any resources known at this time to be required. For example, for a quality review, at least the chair and presenter should be known, and possibly some of the reviewers. When a Team Plan is created for a Work Package, other reviewers may be identified, and these are also added to the Quality Register. When the quality check is done (*Execute a Work Package*), the actual date is added with details of how many errors were found and the target date for correction. Finally, the date of actual completion is added when the product is accepted.

14.7.1 Stage Quality Activities

Each Stage plan contains lower level detail than the Quality Management Strategy. This identifies the method of quality checking to be used for each product of the stage. The plan also identifies responsibilities for each individual quality check. For example, for each quality review the chair and reviewers are identified. This gives an opportunity for those with Project Assurance roles to see each draft Stage Plan and input their needs for checking and the staff who should represent them at each check.

14.8 PRODUCT DESCRIPTIONS

Product Descriptions are created as part of Product-based Planning.

A Product Description should be written for each major product to be produced by the project.

The Product Description should be written as soon as possible after the need for it is recognized. At the start, it may only be possible to create a skeleton of a Product Description, to be completed as more information becomes available. Writing the full description helps the planner understand what the product is and how long it is likely to take to build it.

The Product Description is also the first place where we start thinking about the quality of the product, how we will test the presence of its quality and who we might need in order to test that quality.

It is very sensible to get the customer to write as much of the Product Description as possible, particularly the product's purpose and quality criteria. This helps the customer define what is needed and is useful when delivering a product to be able to confirm that a product meets its quality criteria.

Product Descriptions form an important part of the information handed to a Team Manager as part of a Work Package.

Any time that a product approved by the Project Board has to be changed, the Product Description should also be checked to see if it needs an update.

14.9 QUALITY REVIEW

This is a method of checking a document's quality by a team review. The purpose of a quality review is to inspect a product for errors in a planned, independent, controlled and documented manner and ensure that any errors found are fixed. It needs to be used with common sense to avoid the dangers of an over-bureaucratic approach but with the intent to follow the procedures laid down (to ensure nothing is missed).

Quality review documentation, together with the Quality Register, provides a record that the product was inspected, that any errors found were corrected and that the corrections were themselves checked. Knowing that a product has been checked and declared error-free provides a more confident basis to move ahead and use that product as the basis of future work.

14.9.1 People Involved

The interests of parties who should be *considered* when drawing up the list of attendees are:

- The product author;
- Those with Project Assurance responsibilities delegated by the Project Board;

- The customer;
- Staff who will operate or maintain the finished product;
- Other staff whose work will be affected by the product;
- Specialists in the relevant product area;
- Standards representatives.

14.9.2 Roles at the Quality Review

The roles involved in a quality review are:

- The **presenter**, who is normally the author of the product being reviewed. This role has to ensure that the reviewers have all the required information in order to carry out the review. This means getting a copy of the product from the Configuration Librarian to them during the preparation phase, plus any other documents needed to put it in context. Then the presenter has to answer questions about the product during the review until a decision can be reached on whether there are errors. Finally, the presenter will do most, if not all, of the correcting work. The presenter should not be defensive about the product.
- The **chair**, responsible for ensuring that the quality review is properly organized and that it runs smoothly during all of its phases.
- **Reviewers**, people who have either a vested interest in the quality of the product or who have the skills and experience necessary to assess the quality of the product.
- An **administrator**, someone to take notes of the actions identified at the meeting.

It must be remembered that these are roles. They must all be present at a quality review, but a person may take on more than one role.

14.9.3 Quality Review Phases

There are three distinct phases within the quality review procedure: preparation, review and follow-up.

Phase 1: Preparation

The objective of this phase is to examine the product under review and to create a list of questions for the review.

The chair checks that the product is ready for review and ensures that arrangements for the review are made. This may be delegated to the administrator. The chair also checks that the planned reviewers are available.

The presenter distributes copies of the product and its Product Description to the reviewers.

Each reviewer will study the product and supporting documents (including the quality criteria included in the Product Description), annotate the product and complete a question list.

The chair creates an agenda for the review from the question lists in discussion with the presenter.

Phase 2: Review

The chair makes any necessary introductions and invites reviewers to expand on their questions, based on the agenda. The presenter leads any discussion to answer the questions. The chair ensures that discussions stay focused on the product, do not become repetitive and any errors identified are added to a follow-up action list by the administrator.

The objective of the review is to agree upon a list of any actions needed to correct or complete the product. The chair and the presenter do not have to reconcile these actions at the meeting; it is sufficient for the chair and reviewers to agree that a particular area needs correction or at least reexamination. Provided that the action is logged by the administrator on a follow-up action list, the reviewers have an opportunity in the next phase to confirm that action has been taken.

At the end of the review, the chair invites the administrator to read back the list of follow-up actions and agreement is reached on who will do the corrective work, by when and who will check the change. The actual date of the quality check, a summary of the results and planned dates for any corrections and sign-off should be passed to Project Support to be added to the Quality Register.

Finally, the chair advises the Project Manager and Team Manager of the result.

Phase 3: Follow-Up

The objective of the follow-up phase is to ensure that all actions identified on the action list are dealt with. Actions are coordinated by the presenter.

When an error has been fixed, the presenter will obtain sign-off from whoever is nominated on the action list. This person may be the reviewer who raised the query initially, but other reviewers have the option of checking the correction.

When all errors have been reconciled and sign-off obtained, the chair will confirm to the Project Manager that the product is complete and sign off on the action list. The documents will be filed in the quality file by the administrator and the Stage Plan and Quality Register updated by Project Support.

All documents relating to a quality check should be kept in a quality file to support entries in the Quality Register and any quality audits.

14.9.4 Formal and Informal Reviews

Quality reviews can be either formal (i.e. a scheduled meeting conducted as described above) or informal (e.g. a 'get-together' between two people to informally review a product).

Informal quality reviews will follow a similar format to the formal quality review – the paperwork emerging from both meetings is similar. The main difference will be the number of people involved, the informality of the proceedings during the three phases and the overall time required.

Chapter 15

Risk

15.1 PHILOSOPHY

A risk is an event or a combination of events that may or may not occur, but if they do, they will have an effect on achievement of the project's objectives. This means that risk management is a prerequisite to the PRINCE2 principle of continued business justification.

A risk may be a threat or an opportunity.

Every project is subject to constant change in its business and wider environment. The risk environment is constantly changing too. The project's priorities and relative importance of risks will shift and change. Assumptions about risk have to be regularly revisited and reconsidered, e.g. at each end-stage assessment.

The purpose of the Risk theme is to identify, assess and control any uncertainties in order to improve the project's chances of success.

Risk management should be proactive and systematic.

15.2 RISK MANAGEMENT STRATEGY

This describes the procedures to be used to identify, record, analyse and control risks. Risks can arise at any time, but there are also defined moments when the risk situation should be examined. The strategy should cover both situations.

A Risk Management Strategy should be created for a project as part of *Initiating a Project*. Any corporate or programme risk management policies or guides should be sought out and checked for application to the project.

15.2.1 Risk Tolerance

Another name for this is 'risk appetite'. An important piece of information at creation of the Risk Management Strategy is how much risk the Project Board is willing to take in the project. For example, a project to build a new chemical factory would have a very low 'risk appetite', whereas in wartime a project to capture a strategic bridge may have a very high 'risk appetite'.

Risk Tolerance can be related to the other tolerance parameters: risks to completion within timescale and/or cost, risks to achieving product quality and project scope and risks to achieving the benefits defined in the Business Case.

The organization's overall tolerance of exposure to risk must also be considered as well as a view of individual risks.

15.2.2 Risk Register

A project should record risk details in a Risk Register. Procedures for maintaining this are part of the Risk Management Strategy.

Details of the suggested contents of a Risk Register can be found in Appendix A.

Until the Risk Register is created during initiation, any discovered risks should be recorded in the Daily Log and then transferred over on creation of the register.

15.2.3 Risk Management Times

PRINCE2 suggests that you:

- Carry out risk assessment at the start of a project. Make proposals on what should be done about the risks. Get agreement on whether to start the project or not. Risk assessment is done during *Starting up a Project* (risks in the project mandate, the initiation Stage Plan, the Project Approach etc). As there is no Risk Register yet, details of identified risks are kept in the Daily Log. Risk management is also done as part of *Initiating a Project*. The Risk Register is now available, so any risks recorded in the Daily Log can be transferred.

- Appoint an owner for every risk. Build into a Stage Plan (or put a reminder in the Daily Log) the moments when the owners should be monitoring the risks. Check with the owners that they are doing the job and keeping the risk status up-to-date.
- Review every issue for its impact on existing risks or the creation of a new risk. Build the time and cost of any risk avoidance or reduction into your recommendation on the action to be taken.
- Review the risks at the end of every stage. This includes existing risks that might have changed and new risks caused by the next Stage Plan.
- Inspect the risks at the end of the project for any that might affect the product in its operational life. If there are any, make sure that you notify those charged with looking after the product. (Use the follow-on action recommendations for this.)

15.2.4 Risk Responsibilities

The Project Manager has the responsibility to ensure that risks are identified, recorded and regularly reviewed. The Project Board has the following responsibilities:
Executive:
- Ensure that a Risk Management Strategy is created;
- Ensure that risks associated with the Business Case are identified, assessed and controlled;
- Escalate risks, if sufficiently serious, to corporate or programme management.
Senior User:
- Ensure that risks to the user community are identified, assessed and controlled (risks affecting benefits, operational use or maintenance).
Senior Supplier:
- Ensure that risks to the creation of products or the supplier's interests are identified, assessed and controlled.

15.2.5 Early Warning Indicators

These are thresholds or levels of items that can be monitored to give advanced warning that a risk situation might be developing. Examples are:

- The number of issues being raised;
- The number of quality review errors;
- The amount behind schedule;
- The amount overspent.

15.3 THE RISK MANAGEMENT PROCEDURE

The risk management procedure has five steps as shown in Figure 15.1:

- Identify;
- Assess;
- Plan;
- Implement;
- Communicate.

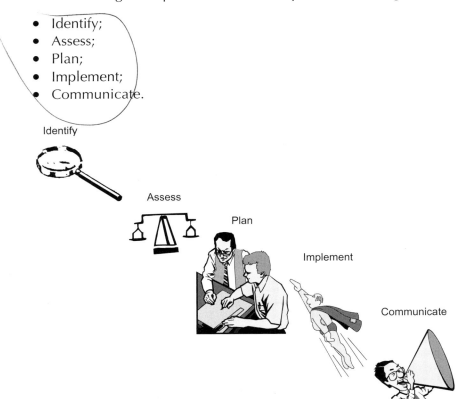

FIGURE 15.1 The five steps in the management of risk.

15.3.1 Identify Risks

This step identifies the potential risks (or opportunities) facing the project. It is important not to judge the likelihood of a risk at this early time.

- Identify critical parts of the project. Note potential sources of risk for these parts. Prepare early warning indicators for these.
- Identify risks and record them in the Risk Register.
- Review captured risks with stakeholders.

Risk Cause, Event and Effect

It is easy to confuse a risk cause with its impact. PRINCE2 offers a useful way of expressing risks in an unambiguous manner. This breaks a risk into its three parts:

- Risk cause;
- Risk event;
- Risk effect.

An example of this way of defining a risk might be:

> 'the new drink/drive laws (*risk cause*) might reduce the number of diners prepared to come to our country restaurant (*risk event*), which would badly affect our cash flow (*risk effect*)'.

15.3.2 Assess

Risk assessment is concerned with the probability, proximity and impact of individual risks, taking into account any interdependencies or other factors outside the immediate scope under investigation.

- *Probability* is the likelihood of a particular outcome actually happening (including a consideration of the frequency with which the outcome may arise).

- *Proximity*: When considering a risk's probability, another aspect is when the risk might occur. Some risks will be predicted to be further away in time than others, and so attention can be focused on the more immediate ones. This prediction is called the risk's proximity. The proximity of each risk should be included in the Risk Register.
- *Impact* is the effect or result of a particular outcome actually happening. For example, occasional personal computer system failure is fairly likely to happen, but would not usually have a major impact on the business. Conversely, loss of power to a building is relatively unlikely to happen, but would have enormous impact on business continuity. As part of this, there should be an understanding of how the impact may change over the life of the project.

Summary Risk Profile

A graphical way of viewing risks is in a summary risk profile. An example is shown in Figure 15.2. This puts risks, using their unique identifiers, in a table of low to high probability and impact. In the example, the top right-hand corner contains risks with a high probability and high impact. The thick black line shows the risk tolerance level, so any risks to the right of that are beyond the risk tolerance levels. Such a

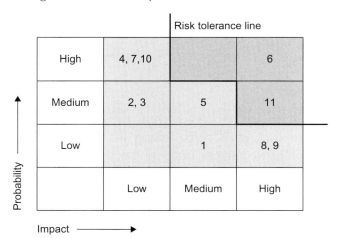

FIGURE 15.2 Summary risk profile.

table is a snapshot of known risks at a certain time and would need to be updated regularly. Updating it may show trends in known risks.

15.3.3 Plan

This involves selection of a risk response from a range of actions. For each possible action it is a question of balancing the cost of taking that action against the likelihood and impact of allowing the risk to occur (Figure 15.3).

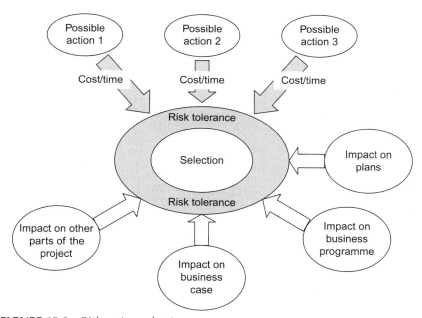

FIGURE 15.3 Risk action selection.

The consideration has to be done in the light of the risk tolerances.

It can be useful to look at previous projects' Lesson Reports to see what risks were considered, what responses were selected and whether the responses were effective.

Table 15.1   Risk Responses

Avoid (threat)	Terminate the risk – by doing things differently and thus removing the risk, where it is feasible to do so. Counter-measures are put in place that either stop the threat or problem from occurring, or prevent it from having any impact on the project or business.
Reduce (threat)	Treat the risk – take action to control it in some way where the actions either reduce the likelihood of the risk developing or limit the impact on the project to acceptable levels.
Transfer (threat)	This is a specialist form of risk reduction where the financial impact of the risk is passed to a third party via, for instance, an insurance policy or a liquidated damage clause.
Accept (threat)	Tolerate the risk – perhaps because nothing can be done at a reasonable cost to mitigate it, or the likelihood and impact of the risk occurring are at an acceptable level. Such threats should continue to be monitored.
Fallback (threat)	These are actions planned and organised to come into force as and when the risk occurs.
Share (threat or opportunity)	Both parties agree on the likely costs and share any savings or extra costs on either side of this figure.
Exploit (opportunity)	Take action to ensure the opportunity does occur and the positive impact is achieved.
Enhance (opportunity)	Work to improve the chances of the opportunity to arise and to enhance the benefits gained from its occurrence.
Reject (opportunity)	A decision not to take the opportunity (at this time) because of other considerations. Such opportunities should continue to be monitored.

The actions can be divided broadly into five types of threat response, three types of response to opportunities and one type common to both threat and opportunity (Table 15.1).

Results of the risk planning are documented in the Risk Register. If the project is part of a programme, project risks should be examined for any impact on the programme (and vice versa). Where any cross-impact is found, the risk should be added to the other Risk Register.

15.3.4 Implement

Having made the selection, the implementation will need planning and resourcing, and is likely to include plan changes and new or modified Work Packages.

There must be mechanisms in place for monitoring and reporting the risk actions.

Some of the actions may only be to monitor the identified risk for signs of a change in its status.

Risk Owner

It is good practice to appoint one individual as responsible for monitoring each identified risk, the person best placed to observe the factors that affect that risk. According to the risk, this person may be a member of the Project Board, someone with Project Assurance duties, the Project Manager, Team Manager or a team member.

Risk Actionee

This is a term used to describe a person assigned to carry out a risk response action.

15.3.5 Communicate

Risks owned at team level should be reported on in the Checkpoint Reports. The Project Manager includes some form of report on any significant risks in the Highlight Report. The End Stage Report also summarizes the risk status. Where a risk actually occurs, an issue should be raised to trigger the necessary actions. There may also be open risks at the end of a project that should be passed to those operating and maintaining the product.

Are there any risks that should be noted in the Lessons Log?

15.4 RISK BUDGET

A risk budget is a sum of money set aside at initiation time to cover responses to a project's threats and opportunities, such as fallback plans. Apart from the risks known at the start of a project, it is always prudent to make provision for risks that are as yet unknown.

15.5 MAPPING THE RISK MANAGEMENT THEME TO THE PRINCE2 THEMES AND PROCESSES

At key points in a project, management of risk should be carried out (Figure 15.4).

15.5.1 Assemble the Project Brief (SU)

The project mandate may have referred to a number of risks facing the potential project. These may be such risks as competitor action, impending or mooted legislation, company policy changes, staff reorganization or cash-flow problems. The preparation of the Project Brief should cause an early study of such risks. Creation of the project approach may also have introduced some extra risks. These should be captured in the Daily Log until the Risk Register is created.

15.5.2 Authorize Initiation (DP)

This is the first formal moment when the Project Board can examine the risks recorded in the Daily Log as part of deciding whether project initiation can be justified. Pragmatically, the Project Manager should have discussed informally with board members any known risks that seem to threaten the project viability.

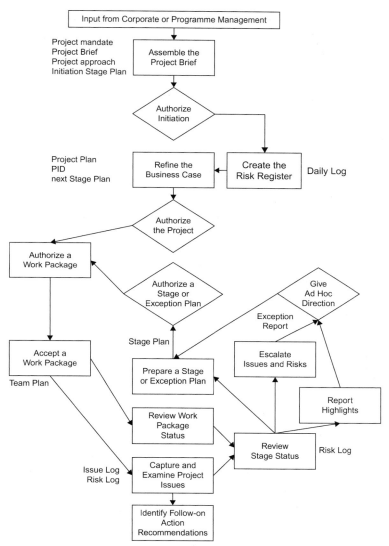

FIGURE 15.4 Mapping risk management to the themes and processes.

15.5.3 Create the Risk Register (IP)

The Project Manager creates the Risk Register and transfers any existing risks to it from the Daily Log.

15.5.4 Refine the Business Case (IP)

The Project Manager examines risks again as part of refining the Business Case. There may be a number of risks in achieving some of the benefits.

15.5.5 Authorize a Project (DP)

The Project Board now has an updated Risk Register to examine as part of its decision on whether to go ahead with the project. As a result of refining the Business Case, a number of business risks may have been identified. Very often the 'owners' of these risks will be members of the Project Board, and they should confirm their ownership and the actions required of them.

15.5.6 Managing a Stage Boundary (SB)

Each time that a plan is produced, elements of the plan may identify new risks, modify existing ones or eliminate others. No plan should be put forward for approval before its risk content has been analyzed. This analysis may lead to the plan being modified in order to take the appropriate risk action(s). The Risk Register should be updated with all such details.

15.5.7 Authorize a Stage or Exception Plan (DP)

Before authorizing a plan, the Project Board has the opportunity to study the risk situation as part of its judgment of the continuing viability of the project.

15.5.8 Authorize a Work Package (CS)

Negotiation with the Team Manager or team member may identify new risks or change old ones. It may require the Project Manager to go back and amend some part of the original Work Package or change the Stage Plan. Examples here are the assignee seeking more time or needing to change resources.

15.5.9 Accept a Work Package (MP)

This is the point when the Team Manager makes out a Team Plan to ensure that the products of the Work Package can be delivered within the constraints of the agreed Work Package. Like any other plan, it may contain new risks or modify existing ones.

15.5.10 Capture and Examine Issues (CS)

Assessment of a new issue may throw up a risk situation. This may stem from either the technical impact analysis or the business impact analysis. For example, the proposed change may produce a risk of pushing the stage or project beyond its tolerance margins.

15.5.11 Review Stage Status (CS)

This brings together the Stage Plan with its latest actual figures, the Project Plan, the Business Case, open issues, the tolerance status and the Risk Register. The Project Manager (in conjunction with the Project Assurance roles) looks for risk situation changes as well as any other warning signs.

15.5.12 Escalate Issues and Risks (CS)

As well as issues, a risk change may cause the Project Manager to raise an Exception Report to the Project Board.

15.5.13 Report Highlights (CS)

As part of this task, the Project Manager may take the opportunity to raise any risk matters with the Project Board. Examples here would be notifying the board of any risks that are no longer relevant, warning about new risks and sending reminders about business risks that board members should be keeping an eye on. The suggested format of a Highlight Report is included in Appendix A Product Description outlines.

15.5.14 Give Ad Hoc Direction (DP)

The Project Manager advises the Project Board of exception situations via the Exception Report. It has the opportunity to react with advice or a decision, e.g., bringing the project to a premature close, requesting an Exception Plan or removing the problem. The Project Board may instigate ad hoc advice on the basis of information given to it from corporate or programme management or another external source.

15.5.15 Hand Over Products (CP)

At the end of the project a number of risks may have been identified that will affect the product in its operational life. These should be transferred to the follow-on action recommendations for the information of those who will support the product after the project.

Chapter 16

Change

The Change theme covers change control and configuration management.

16.1 CONFIGURATION MANAGEMENT

16.1.1 Philosophy

No organization can be fully efficient or effective unless it manages its assets, particularly if the assets are vital to the running of the organization's business. A project's assets likewise have to be managed. The assets of the project are the products that it develops. The name for the combined set of these assets is a configuration. The configuration of the final deliverable of a project is the sum total of its products.

16.1.2 Purpose

The purpose of configuration management is to identify, track and protect the project's products as they are developed.

16.1.3 Configuration Management Strategy

During initiation, a Configuration Management Strategy should be written. This covers both configuration management and change control.

The first step in this is to check if there are corporate or programme policies and procedures that cover this area.

The contents of a Configuration Management Strategy are:

- Procedures covering the identification of products, where master copies are to be kept and how they are to be controlled, status accounting and configuration auditing;
- The Issue and Change Control procedures;
- Configuration management and change control responsibilities;
- Record retention;
- Reporting on the performance of the procedures;
- The timing of change control and configuration management activities;
- Any tools, software or techniques to be used.

Configuration management is closely linked to the management of changes to the project's products. It must be possible to retrieve any version of a product at any time and any revision of the components that make up that product. Configuration management must ensure that the resulting product will always be built in an identical manner. Product enhancements and special variants create the need to control multiple versions and releases of the product. All these have to be handled by configuration management.

16.1.4 Baselines

Baselines are moments in a product's development when it and all its components have reached an acceptable state, such that they can be 'frozen' and used as a base for the next step. The next step may be to release the product to the customer, or it may be that you have 'frozen' a design and will now construct the products from that design.

So, in summary, a baseline is created for one of a number of reasons:

- To provide a sound base for future work;
- As a point to which you can retreat if development goes wrong;
- As an indication of the component and version numbers of a release;

- As a bill of material showing the variants released to a specific site;
- To copy the products and documentation at the current baseline to all remote sites;
- To represent a standard configuration (e.g. Product Description) against which supplies can be obtained (e.g. purchase of personal computers for a group);
- To transfer configuration items to another library, e.g. from development to production, from the supplier to the customer at the end of the project.

16.1.5 Product Status Account

Product status accounting provides a complete statement of the current status and history of the products generated within the project or within a stage.

One use for a Product Status Account is for a Project Manager to check that all stage products have been completed and approved at a stage end. Another use is for configuration auditing.

There are two purposes of configuration auditing:

- The first is to confirm that the Configuration Item Records match reality. In other words, if Configuration Item Records show that we are developing version 3 of a product, you want to be sure that the developer has not moved on to version 5 without your knowledge and without any linking documentation to say why versions 4 and 5 were created.
- The second purpose is to account for any differences between a delivered product and its original agreed specification. In other words, can the Configuration Item Records trace a path from the original specification through any approved changes to what a product looks like now? These audits should verify that:
  1. All authorized versions of configuration items exist.
  2. Only authorized configuration items exist.
  3. All change records and release records have been properly authorized by project management.
  4. Implemented changes are as authorized.

16.2 CHANGE CONTROL

16.2.1 Philosophy of Change

Change is inevitable during the life of a project. No matter how well planned a project has been, if there is no control over changes, this will destroy any chance of completing the project on schedule and within budget.

16.2.2 Change Authority

As part of the Configuration Management Strategy the Project Board must decide if it wishes to delegate some authority for approving or rejecting requests for change or off-specifications. This depends on factors such as the number of requests expected, the technical nature of the requests and availability of the Project Board members to look at the requests.

The Project Board should define a scale of importance for changes to identify those which should be handled by:

- Corporate or programme management;
- The Project Board;
- A Change Authority;
- The Project Manager.

If a Change Authority is appointed, it should be given a change budget together with any constraints on its use, such as maximum cost of a single change, maximum budget for a single stage.

16.2.3 Issues and Types of Issue

In PRINCE2 an issue is the formal way of recording any inquiry, complaint or request into a project. It can be raised by anyone associated with the project about anything, e.g.:

- A desired new or changed function;
- A failure of a product in meeting some aspect of the user requirements;

- A concern in the mind of someone connected with the project;
- A problem.

In other words, there is no limit to the content of an issue beyond the fact that it should be about the project.

All possible changes should be handled by the same change control procedure. Apart from controlling possible changes, this procedure should provide a formal entry point through which questions or suggestions also can be raised and answered.

All issues have to be closed by the end of the project or transferred to the follow-on action recommendations. The transfer of an issue to these recommendations can only be done with the approval of the Project Board.

16.2.4 Request for Change

A request for change records a proposed modification to a baseline.

16.2.5 Off-Specification

An off-specification is used to document any situation where something that was expected is forecast not to be provided. Examples might be a missing product or the product is failing to meet its specification in some respect.

16.2.6 Problem or Concern

An issue may be simply a question or a general concern expressed by someone.

16.3 PROCEDURE FOR ISSUE AND CHANGE CONTROL

PRINCE2 provides a structured set of procedures to identify, analyze and control changes.

There are five steps in the Change Control procedure:

- Capture;
- Examine;
- Propose;
- Decide;
- Implement.

16.3.1 Capture

This is a brief analysis of the issue to determine its type and whether it should be handled formally or informally.

The purpose of this analysis is to:

- Ensure decisions on issues are made at the correct level – Project Manager, Project Board or corporate/programme management;
- Protect the Project Board as much as possible from having to make decisions on trivial matters;
- Reduce the need for formal documentation as much as possible.

Issues that need to be managed formally are transferred to an Issue Report, given a unique identifier and entered on the Issue Register.

If an issue is a problem or concern, this may not require formal handling. The Project Manager may decide to deal with it directly. A note of the problem/concern and any action taken should be made in the Daily Log. If a later decision is made that the issue requires to be handled formally, it is transferred to an Issue Report and entered on the Issue Register.

16.3.2 Examine

Impact analysis is done to find out:

- What would have to change;
- What would be the impact on other products;

- The estimated time and cost;
- Any impact on quality;
- Any impact on the project scope;
- Business Case impact;
- Impact on risks.

If the project is part of a programme, the issue should be analyzed for any impact at that level.

After this analysis, the priority of the issue should be reevaluated.

The Issue Register and Issue Report are then updated with this information.

16.3.3 Propose

Alternative responses are considered and a selection made, balancing the costs and risks of the response against the value of the change.

16.3.4 Decide

The Project Manager may be able to decide on some minor issues if they can be handled within the Stage Plan. If so, permission for this should have been documented in the Configuration Management Strategy. *Remember that tolerances are not there to pay for requests for change.*

Other Issue Reports should go to the Project Board or Change Authority for decision. Where the selected response would cause an exception outside tolerances, an Exception Report would be escalated to the Project Board.

The Project Board's decision may be to:

- Implement the change. This means asking the Project Manager to create an Exception Plan;
- Delay the change to an enhancement project after the current one is finished;

- Defer a decision until a later meeting;
- Ask for more information;
- Cancel the request.

The decision should be documented on the Issue Report and in the Issue Register.

16.3.5 Implement

This will take the form of either a new or a modified Work Package, or create an Exception Plan for approval by the Project Board (see the Progress chapter for more details).

Chapter 17

Tailoring PRINCE2 to the Project Environment

There are two terms that can be confused: 'tailoring PRINCE2' and 'embedding PRINCE2'. Tailoring refers to any adjustment to the PRINCE2 method for a specific project in terms of the project's

- Scale,
- Complexity,
- Geography,
- Culture,

and whether the project is part of a programme.

Embedding refers to the adoption of PRINCE2 across a business.

17.1 TAILORING IS NOT

-dropping parts of the method. The processes and themes are inter-linked throughout the method. Any isolated decision to drop a process or a theme will result in a flawed use of the system and may cause project failure.

17.2 TAILORING IS

-adopting the method to factors such as existing standards, documentation and procedures of the business. For example, the business may already have a change control procedure and set of documents

153

to support it that it wants to use. A project may be so small that it is sensible to combine Team Plans into the Stage Plan. It may make sense to combine two or more of the PRINCE2 roles for a given project.

17.3 ADAPTATION

Most adaptation questions come from those who wish to use the method on small projects, but view the full method as too bureaucratic. The key question is: 'How much of this theme, process or technique do we need to use for this project?'.

17.3.1 Principles

The PRINCE2 principles should always be applied.

17.3.2 Themes

It may be that the business has standards in certain areas of project work that it wishes to retain: contractual, organizational, change control, quality, risk management, configuration management and so on. It may be that a project is too small to need the full weight offered by a PRINCE2 theme. The Project Manager must understand the PRINCE2 method and be able to judge at what level each theme needs to be used.

Business Case. There should always be justification for a project, however small. It may only be the reasons for doing the project, but there should always be understanding that the benefits from a project outweigh the cost.

Organization. This theme may be the most affected when tailoring, especially for simple projects. All the responsibilities are needed, whatever the size of project. It is just a question of who should take which role or roles. In simple projects it may be sensible to combine roles, such as Executive and Senior User. The Project Board members may do their own Project Assurance. The Project Manager may also pick up the Project Support role. A team member may also act as configuration librarian.

In a large project, several people may need to share the role of the Senior User or the Senior Supplier. A team of people may be required to perform the Project Assurance role for the Senior User.

PRINCE2 does not recommend sharing the role of Project Manager, nor that of the Executive, but if the project is partly or wholly funded by someone other than the customer, even the role of the Executive may be shared. An example of this in the United Kingdom would be PFI (Private Finance Initiative), where the supplier provides the funding and takes profits from the use of the outcome.

The most common example of sharing project roles is where the project is part of a programme, and someone from the programme management team also takes a place on the Project Board.

More About Project-Programme Organization Tailoring

The Executives of the projects within a programme would sit on the programme board to improve communications and decision-making. The Business Change Manager of a programme, responsible for benefits definition, may take a role as the Senior User in one or more of the programme's projects. Project Support may be handled by the programme for all its projects. A programme's design authority may have a role in the Change Authority or Project Assurance of one or more of its projects.

Plans. In a small project there are a number of possibilities. The Project Plan, Stage Plans and Team Plans may be combined into one plan if this gives enough detail to provide control on a day-to-day basis. It may be acceptable to use a single Product Checklist instead of drawing a Product Breakdown Structure, Product Flow Diagram, network plan and Gantt chart. (See the Quality section below about Product Descriptions.)

Quality. Great care is needed when thinking of scaling down the quality work described in PRINCE2. It is strongly recommended

that Product Descriptions for the key products are written, whatever the size of project. It may be enough to keep a record of the
quality checks in the Daily Log.

Risk. Risk is present in every project, large or small. The risk activities defined in the risk theme can be done far more informally than
for medium or large projects, but they should always be done.

Configuration Management. There should always be an identification scheme and a simple form of version control.

Change Control. Even in the smallest of projects changes will
occur and should be recorded. The procedure can be simplified,
but must be done.

Progress. Some form of progress control and reporting is required,
however simple. Full Checkpoint and Highlight Reports, even End
Stage Reports, may not be required and reports can be oral, rather
than written.

17.3.3 Processes

All the processes should be used to some extent. In a programme
environment, where a lot of start-up information is provided to the
project, it may be acceptable to combine the *'Starting up a Project'*
and *'Initiating a Project'* processes. In a small project it may be possible to combine the processes of *'Controlling a Stage'* and *'Managing
Product Delivery'*.

Product Descriptions

This appendix contains Product Description outlines for PRINCE2's management products. These are not full Product Descriptions as defined by the description of a 'Product Description' (see Section A.16) as some elements, such as quality method, will vary depending on the project's needs. Format examples are provided; however, these are not exhaustive. The contents of these outline Product Descriptions should be tailored to the requirements and environment of each project.

A.1 BENEFITS REVIEW PLAN

A.1.1 Purpose

A Benefits Review Plan defines how and when a measurement of the achievement of the project's expected benefits can be made.

A.1.2 Composition

- What benefits are to be measured?
- Who is accountable for achievement of the expected benefits?
- How and when achievement of expected benefits can be measured?
- What resources are needed for the review work?
- Baseline measurements from which improvements will be calculated.

A.1.3 Derivation

- Business Case;
- Project Product Description (acceptance criteria);
- The programme's benefit realization plan (if part of a programme).

A.1.4 Format and Presentation

- Document, spreadsheet or presentation slides.

A.1.5 Quality Criteria

- It covers all benefits mentioned in the Business Case.
- The benefits are measurable and baseline measures have been recorded.
- It describes suitable timing for measurement of the benefits, together with reasons for the timing.
- It identifies the skills or individuals who will be needed to carry out the measurements.
- The effort and cost to undertake the benefit reviews are realistic when compared to the value of the anticipated benefits.
- Consideration is given to whether any negative benefits should be measured and reviewed.

A.2 BUSINESS CASE

A.2.1 Purpose

A Business Case is used to document the justification for the undertaking of a project, based on the estimated costs of development, implementation, operation and maintenance against the anticipated business benefits to be gained.

A.2.2 Composition

- Executive Summary: Highlights the key points in the Business Case, which should include important benefits and the return on investment;

- Reasons: Defines the reasons for undertaking the project;
- Business Options: Description and summary analysis of the business options considered (do nothing, do minimal or do something) and the reasoned selection;
- Expected Benefits: The benefits that the project will deliver expressed in measurable terms against the situation as it exists prior to the project;
- Expected Negative Benefits: Outcomes perceived as negative by one or more stakeholders;
- Timescale: Summary of the Project Plan timescale and the period over which the benefits will be realized;
- Costs: A summary of the project costs (taken from the Project Plan) and the on-going operations/maintenance costs;
- Investment Appraisal: Compares the aggregated benefits to the project costs and the ongoing incremental operations and maintenance costs;
- Major Risks: Gives a summary of the key risks associated with the project together with the likely impact and plans should they occur.

A.2.3 Derivation

- Project Mandate and Project Brief – reasons;
- Project Plan – costs and timescales;
- The Senior User(s) – expected benefits;
- The Executive – value for money;
- Risk Register;
- Issue Register.

A.2.4 Format and Presentation

A Business Case can take a number of formats, including:

- Document, spreadsheet or presentation slides.

A.2.5 Quality Criteria

- The reasons for the project must be consistent with corporate or programme strategy.

- The Project Plan and Business Case must be aligned.
- The benefits should be clearly identified and justified.
- It should be clear how the benefits will be realized.
- It should be clear what will define a successful outcome.
- It should be clear what the preferred business option is and why.
- It should be clear how any necessary funding will be obtained.
- The Business Case includes operations and maintenance costs/ risks as well as project costs/risks.
- The major risks faced by the project are explicitly stated together with any proposed responses.

A.3 CHECKPOINT REPORT

A.3.1 Purpose

A Checkpoint Report is used to report the status of the Work Package.

A.3.2 Composition

- Date: The date of the checkpoint;
- Period: The reporting period covered by the Checkpoint Report;
- Follow-ups: From previous reports, e.g. action items completed, issues outstanding;
- This Reporting Period:
  1. The products being developed by the team during the reporting period,
  2. The products completed by the team during the reporting period,
  3. Quality management activities carried out during the period,
  4. Lessons identified;
- Next Reporting Period:
  1. The products being developed by the team in the next reporting period,
  2. The products planned to be completed by the team in the next reporting period,
  3. Quality management activities planned for the next reporting period;

- Work Package Tolerance Status: How execution of the Work Package is performing against its tolerances (e.g. cost/time/scope actuals and forecast);
- Issues and Risks: Updates on issues and risks associated with the Work Package.

A.3.3 Derivation

- Work Package;
- Team Plan and actuals;
- Previous checkpoint.

A.3.4 Format and Presentation

A Checkpoint Report can take a number of formats, including:

- Verbal report to the Project Manager;
- Presentation at a progress review;
- Document or email issued to the Project Manager.

A.3.5 Quality Criteria

- It is prepared at the frequency defined in the Work Package.
- Every product in the Work Package for that period is covered by the report.
- It includes an update on any unresolved issues from the previous report.

A.4 COMMUNICATION MANAGEMENT STRATEGY

A.4.1 Purpose

A Communication Management Strategy contains a description of the means and frequency of communication between the project team, stakeholders and other interested parties.

A.4.2 Composition

- Introduction: States the purpose, objectives, scope and owner of the strategy;
- Communication Process: A description of any communication methods to be used; any variance from corporate or programme management standards should be highlighted, together with a justification for the variance;
- Tools and Techniques: Any communication tools to be used and any preference for techniques that may be used;
- Records: What communication records will be required and where they will be stored;
- Reporting: Any reports that are to be produced, their purpose and recipients (e.g. performance indicators);
- Timing of Communication Activities: States when formal communication activities are to be undertaken;
- Roles and Responsibilities: Describes who will be responsible for specific aspects of the communication process;
- Stakeholder analysis;
- Identification of each interested party;
- Current relationship;
- Desired relationship;
- Interfaces;
- Key messages;
- Information needs for each interested party;
- Information required to be provided from the project;
- Information required to be provided to the project;
- Information provider and recipient;
- Frequency of communication;
- Means of communication;
- Format of the communication.

A.4.3 Derivation

- Corporate communications policies (e.g. rules for disclosure for publicly listed companies);

- The programme's information management strategy;
- Other components of the Project Initiation Documentation (in particular the project management team structure, the various strategies);
- Stakeholder analysis.

A.4.4 Format and Presentation

A Communication Management Strategy can take a number of formats, including:

- Stand-alone product or a section of the Project Initiation Documentation;
- Document, spreadsheet or mindmap.

A.4.5 Quality Criteria

- All stakeholders and interested parties have been identified and consulted for their communication requirements.
- There is agreement from all stakeholders and interested parties about the content, frequency and method.
- A common standard has been considered.
- The time, effort and resources required to carry out the identified communications have been allowed for in Stage Plans.
- The formality and frequency of communication is reasonable for the project's importance and complexity.
- For projects that are part of a programme, the lines of communication and the reporting structure between project and programme have been made clear in the Communication Management Strategy.

A.5 CONFIGURATION ITEM RECORD

A.5.1 Purpose

To provide a record that describes the status, version and variant of a configuration item and any details of important relationships between that and other configuration items.

A.5.2 Composition

- Project Identifier: A unique reference;
- Item Identifier: A unique reference;
- Title: The name of the product as it appears in the Product Breakdown Structure;
- Current Version: Typically an alpha-numeric value;
- Date of last status change;
- Ownership: The person or group currently responsible for the item;
- Location: Where the item is stored;
- Product Attributes: As defined by the Configuration Management Strategy; these are used to specify a subset of products when producing Product Status Accounts, such as the management stage in which the product is created, type of product (e.g. hardware/software), product destination, etc.;
- Users: The person or the group who will use the product;
- Status: As defined by the Configuration Management Strategy, e.g. pending development, in development, in review, approved, handed over;
- State: As defined by the Product Description, e.g. dismantled machinery, moved machinery and reassembled machinery;
- Producer: The person or team responsible for creating or obtaining the product;
- Date Allocated: To the producer;
- Source: In-house, or purchased from a third-party company;
- Relationship with Other Items: Those products that:
  1. Would be affected if this item changed,
  2. If changed would affect this item;
- Cross-references;
- Issue Reports and risks;
- Documentation that defines requirements, design, build, production and verification for the item (specifically this will include the Product Description).

A.5.3 Derivation

- Configuration Management Strategy;
- Product Breakdown Structure;

- Stage Plan and Work Package;
- Quality Register, Issue Register, Risk Register.

A.5.4 Format and Presentation

The Configuration Item Record can take a number of formats, including:

- Document, spreadsheet or database.

A.5.5 Quality Criteria

- The records reflect the status of the product accurately.
- The records are kept together in a secure location.
- The version number matches the actual product.
- A process exists by which the Configuration Item Record is defined and updated.

A.6 CONFIGURATION MANAGEMENT STRATEGY

A.6.1 Purpose

A Configuration Management Strategy is used to identify how and by whom the project's products will be controlled and protected.

It answers the questions:

- How the products and the various versions and variants of these will be identified
- How and where the project's products will be stored
- What storage and retrieval security will be put in place
- How changes to products will controlled
- Where responsibility for configuration management will lie

A.6.2 Composition

- Introduction: States the purpose, objectives, scope and owner of the strategy;

- Configuration Management Procedure: A description of (or reference to) the configuration management method to be used; any variance from corporate or programme management standards should be highlighted, together with a justification for the variance; the process should cover:
  1. Planning,
  2. Identification – including definition of the coding system to be used,
  3. Control – including storage/retrieval arrangements, change control procedures and product hand-over procedures,
  4. Status Accounting,
  5. Verification and Audit;

  Issue and change control procedure: a description of the issue and change control procedures to be used, covering capturing and examining issues and proposing, deciding and implementing solutions. If the procedure is a general standard within the company, this section may just refer to where the procedures can be found and highlight any variances.
- Tools and Techniques: Refers to any configuration management systems or tools to be used and any techniques that may be used for the configuration management procedure;
- Records: Definition of the composition and format of Configuration Item Records, the Issue Register and Issue Reports;
- Reporting: Describes any Product Status Accounts and Issue Reports that are to be produced, their purpose, timing and recipients;
- Timing of configuration management and issue and change control activities: States when configuration audits are to take place;
- Roles and Responsibilities: Describes who will be responsible for the procedures including any corporate or programme management roles involved with the configuration management of the project's products. Describe whether a Change Authority and change budget will be established.

  Scales for priority and severity: levels defining how requests for change and off-specifications should be prioritized and which level of management can make decisions about them.

A.6.3 Derivation

- Customer's quality expectations;
- Any configuration management software in use or mandated by the user;
- (If applicable) Programme Quality Management Strategy and Information Management Strategy;
- The user's quality management system (QMS);
- The supplier's QMS;
- Specific needs of the project's products and environment;
- Project management team structure (to identify the Configuration Librarian);
- Facilitated workshops and informal discussions.

A.6.4 Format and Presentation

A Configuration Management Strategy can take a number of formats, including:

- Stand-alone document or a section of the Project Initiation Documentation.

A.6.5 Quality Criteria

- The responsibilities are clear and understood by both the user and the supplier.
- The key identifier for project products is defined.
- The method and circumstances of version control are clear.
- The strategy provides the Project Manager with all the product information required.
- The corporate or programme strategy for configuration management has been considered.
- The retrieval system will produce all required information in an accurate, timely and usable manner.
- The project files provide the information necessary for any audit requirements.
- The project files provide the historical records required to support any lessons.

- The chosen configuration management strategy is appropriate for the size and nature of the project.
- Resources are in place to administer the chosen method of configuration management.
- The requirements of the operational group (or similar group to whom the Project Product will be passed should be considered.

A.7 DAILY LOG

A.7.1 Purpose

A Daily Log is used to record problems, required actions or significant events not caught by other PRINCE2 registers. It acts as the project diary for the Project Manager.

A.7.2 Composition

A Daily Log may include:

- Identifier;
- Date of entry;
- Details of the problem, action, event or comment;
- Person responsible;
- Target date;
- Results.

A.7.3 Derivation

Entries are made when the Project Manager or the Team Manager feels it is appropriate in order to log some event. Often entries are based on thoughts, conversations, observations and items from plans for checking.

A.7.4 Format and Presentation

A Daily Log can take a number of formats, including:

- Document or spreadsheet;
- Desk diary or log book;
- Electronic diary/calendars/task lists.

A.7.5 Quality Criteria

- Ensure that the entries are sufficiently documented to be understandable later (a short note might make sense at the time, but will it in several months time?).
- It should not be used as a substitute for any of the project registers, e.g. Issue Reports should be recorded on the Issue Register and risks on the Risk Register when these are available.
- Ensure that the date, person responsible and target date are always filled in.

A.8 END PROJECT REPORT

A.8.1 Purpose

The End Project Report is used at project closure to review how the project performed against the original version of the Project Initiation Documentation. It also allows the:

- Passing on of any lessons that can be usefully applied to other projects;
- Passing of details of unfinished work, ongoing risks or potential product modifications to the group charged with future support of the project's products in their operational life.

A.8.2 Composition

- Project Manager's Report: Summarizing the project's performance;
- Review of the Business Case: Summarizing the validity of the project's Business Case;
  - Benefits achieved to date;
  - Residual benefits expected (post-project);
  - Expected net benefits;
  - Deviations from approved Business Case;
- Review of Project Objectives: Review of how the project performed against its planned targets and tolerances for time, cost, quality, scope, benefits and risk;

- Review of Team Performance: In particular providing recognition for good performance;
  - Review of Products;
  - Quality records: a summary of planned and completed quality activities.
  - Approval Records;
  - Off-specifications: Listing any missing products or products that do not meet the original requirements and confirmation of any concessions granted;
  - Project Product Hand Over: Confirmation by the customer that operations and maintenance functions are ready to receive the products;
  - Follow-on Action Recommendations: Unfinished work, unactioned requests for change, concessions that should be removed and any risks that may affect the product in its operational life;
- Lessons Report: A review of what went well, what went badly and any recommendations for corporate/programme management consideration.

A.8.3 Derivation

- The Project Initiation Documentation;
- Business Case;
- Project Plan;
- Benefits Review Plan;
- Issue Register, Quality Register, Risk Register;
- Lessons Report;
- End Stage Reports (and Exceptions Reports, if applicable).

A.8.4 Format and Presentation

An End Project Report can take a number of formats, including:

- Presentation to the Project Board (physical meeting or conference call);
- Document or email issued to the Project Board.

A.8.5 Quality Criteria

- Any abnormal situations are described, together with their impact.
- At the end of the project, all Issue Reports should either be closed or be the subject of a follow-on action recommendation.
- Any available useful documentation or evidence should accompany the follow-on action recommendations.
- Any appointed Project Assurance roles agree with the report.

A.9 END STAGE REPORT

A.9.1 Purpose

An End Stage Report is used to give a summary of progress to date, the overall project situation and sufficient information to ask for a Project Board decision on what to do next with the project.

A.9.2 Composition

- Project Manager's Report: Summarizing the stage performance;
- Review of the Business Case: Summarizing the validity of the project's Business Case;
  - Benefits achieved to date;
  - Residual benefits expected (remaining stages and post-project);
  - Expected net benefits;
  - Deviations from approved Business Case;
- Aggregated risk exposure;
- Review of Project Objectives: Review of how the project has performed to date against its planned targets and tolerances for time, cost, quality, scope, benefits and risk;
- Review of Stage Objectives: Review of how the specific stage performed against its planned targets and tolerances for time, cost, quality, scope, benefits and risk;
- Review of Team Performance: In particular providing recognition for good performance;
- Review of products;
  - Quality Records: A Summary of planned and completed quality activities.

- Approval Records: Listing the products planned for completion in the stage and their requisite approvals;
- Off-specifications: Listing any missing products or products that do not meet the original requirements and confirmation of any concessions granted;
- (If Applicable) Phased Hand Over: Confirmation by the customer that operations and maintenance functions are ready to receive the release;
- (If Appropriate) Lessons Report: A review of what went well, what went badly and any recommendations for corporate/programme management consideration;
- Issues and Risks: Summary of the current set of issues and risks affecting the project;
- Forecast: The Project Manager's forecast for the project and next stage against planned targets and tolerances for time, cost, quality, scope, benefits and risk.

Where the End Stage Report is being produced at the end of the initiation stage, not all of the above content may be appropriate or necessary.

A.9.3 Derivation

- Current Stage Plan and actuals;
- Project Plan;
- Benefits Review Plan;
- Risk Register, Quality Register, Issue Register;
- Exception Report (if applicable);
- Lessons Report;
- Work Packages;
- Updated Business Case.

A.9.4 Format and Presentation

An End Stage Report can take a number of formats, including:

- Presentation to the Project Board (physical meeting or conference call);
- Document or email issued to the Project Board.

A.9.5 Quality Criteria

- The report clearly shows stage performance against the plan.
- Any abnormal situations are described, together with their impact.
- Any appointed Project Assurance roles agree with the report.

A.10 EXCEPTION REPORT

A.10.1 Purpose

An Exception Report is produced when a Stage Plan or Project Plan is forecasted to exceed tolerance levels set. It is prepared by the Project Manager in order to inform the Project Board of the situation and to offer options and recommendations for the way to proceed.

A.10.2 Composition

- Cause of the Exception: A description of the cause of a deviation from the current plan.
- Consequences of the Deviation: What will happen if the deviation is not addressed;
- Options: What are the options that are available to address the deviation and what would be the effect of each option on the Project Plan, Business Case, risks and tolerances;
- Recommendation: Of the available options, what is the recommendation and why.

A.10.3 Derivation

- Current plan and actuals;
- Issue Report;
- Issue Register, Risk Register and Quality Register;
- Project Board advice of an external event that affects the project.

A.10.4 Format and Presentation

An Exception Report can take a number of formats, including:

- Raised at a minuted progress review (physical meeting or conference call);
- Document or email issued to the next higher level of management.

For urgent exceptions, it is recommended that the Exception Report is verbal in the first instance and then followed up in the agreed format.

A.10.5 Quality Criteria

- The current plan must accurately show the status of time and cost.
- The reason(s) for the deviation must be stated, the exception clearly analysed and any impacts assessed and fully described.
- Implications for the Business Case have been considered and the impact on the overall Project Plan has been calculated.
- Options are analysed (including any risks associated with them) and recommendations are made for the most appropriate way to proceed.
- The Exception Report is given in a timely and appropriate manner.

A.11 HIGHLIGHT REPORT

A.11.1 Purpose

A Highlight Report is used to provide the Project Board (and possibly other stakeholders) with a summary of the stage status at intervals defined by them.

A.11.2 Composition

- Date: The date of the report;
- Period: The reporting period covered;

- Status Summary: An overview of the stage status at this time;
- This Reporting Period:
  1. Products completed in the period (if the Work Packages are being performed by external suppliers this information may be accompanied by purchase order and invoicing data);
  2. Products planned but not started or completed in the period (providing early warning indicator or potential breach of time tolerance);
  3. Corrective actions taken during the period.
- Next Reporting Period:
  1. Products to be completed in the next period;
  2. Corrective actions to be completed during the next period.
- Project and Stage Tolerance Status: How the project and stage are performing against their tolerances (e.g. cost/time actuals and forecast);
- Requests for Change: Raised, approved, pending;
- Key Issue Reports and Risks: Summary of actual or potential problems and risks;
- (If Appropriate) Lessons Report: A review of what went well, what went badly and any recommendations for corporate/ programme management consideration.

A.11.3 Derivation

- Project Initiation Documentation;
- Checkpoint Reports;
- Issue Register, Quality Register, Risk Register;
- Stage Plan and actuals.

A.11.4 Format and Presentation

A Highlight Report can take a number of formats, including:

- Presentation to the Project Board (physical meeting or conference call);
- Document or email issued to the Project Board.

A.11.5 Quality Criteria

- The level and frequency of progress reporting required by the Project Board is right for the stage and/or project;
- The information is timely, useful, accurate and objective;
- Highlights any potential problem areas.

A.12 ISSUE REGISTER

A.12.1 Purpose

An Issue Register is used to allocate a unique number to each Issue Report and provide a summary of all the Issue Reports, their type, analysis and status.

A.12.2 Composition

For each entry in the Issue Register, the following should be recorded:

- Issue Identifier: Provides a unique reference for every Issue Report entered into the Issue Register. It will typically be a numeric or an alpha-numeric value;
- Issue Type: Defines the type of Issue Report being recorded, i.e.
  1. problem/concern,
  2. requests for change,
  3. off-specifications;
- Author: The name of the individual or team who raised the Issue Report;
- Date Raised;
- Issue Description: A statement describing the Issue Report, its cause and impact;
- Status: The current status of the Issue Report and the date of last update;
- Priority: In terms of the project's chosen categories.
- Severity: as defined in the Configuration Management Strategy to indicate the level of management required to make a decision on the issue

A.12.3 Derivation

- Entries are initially made on the Issue Register once a new Issue Report has been identified.
- The Issue Register is updated as the Issue Report progresses. Once the Issue Report has been resolved, the entry in the Issue Register is closed.
- Entries on the Issue Register that turn out to be risks should be transferred to the Risk Register and noted in the Issue Register.

A.12.4 Format and Presentation

An Issue Register can take a number of formats, including:

- Document, spreadsheet or database.

The Issue Register may be part of an integrated project register for all risks, actions, decisions, assumptions, Issue Reports, lessons, etc.

A.12.5 Quality Criteria

- The Issue Reports are uniquely identified, including to which product they refer.
- A process is defined to update the Issue Register.
- The Issue Register is kept in a safe place and access to it is controlled.

A.13 ISSUE REPORT

A.13.1 Purpose

- An Issue Report is a report containing the description, impact assessment and recommendations for a request for change, off-specification or a problem/concern. It is only created for those issues that need to be handled formally.

A.13.2 Composition

- Issue Identifier: As shown in the Issue Register (provides a unique reference for every Issue Report);

- Issue Type: Defines the type of Issue Report being recorded, i.e.
  1. Problem/concern,
  2. Request for change,
  3. Off-specification.
- Author: The name of the individual or team who raised the Issue Report;
- Date Raised;
- Issue Description;
- Impact Analysis: A detailed analysis of the likely impact of the issue; this may include, e.g. a list of products impacted;
- Recommendation: What the Project Manager believes should be done to resolve the issue (and why);
- Priority: The priority should be reevaluation after impact analysis;
- Severity: a definition in terms of the severity scales set out in the Configuration Management Strategy to identify the management level required to make a decision on the issue
- Decision: The decision made (accept, reject, defer, grant concession);
- Approved by: Who made the decision;
- Decision Date;
- Closure Date: The date that the Issue Report was closed.

A.13.3 Derivation

- Highlight Report(s), Checkpoint Report(s) and End Stage Report(s);
- Stage Plan with actuals;
- Users and supplier teams working on the project;
- The application of quality controls;
- Observation and experience of the processes;
- Quality Register, Risk Register and Lessons Log;
- Completed Work Packages.

A.13.4 Format and Presentation

An Issue Report can take a number of formats, including:

- Document, spreadsheet or database.

A.13.5 Quality Criteria

- The Issue Report is clear and unambiguous.
- A detailed impact analysis has been done.
- The Issue Report has been examined for its effect on tolerances.
- The Issue Report has been correctly logged on the Issue Register.
- Decisions are accurately and unambiguously described.

A.14 LESSONS LOG

A.14.1 Purpose

The Lessons Log is a repository for lessons that are worth learning for this project or future projects.

A.14.2 Composition

- Lesson Identifier: It provides a unique reference for every lesson entered into the Lessons Log. It will typically be a numeric or an alpha-numeric value.
- Lesson Type: It defines the type of Lesson being recorded, i.e.,
  1. Project – to be applied to this project;
  2. Corporate – to be passed on to corporate;
  3. Both project and corporate.
- Lesson Detail: The detail may include:
  1. Event;
  2. Effect (e.g. positive/negative financial impact);
  3. Causes/trigger;
  4. Whether there were any early warning indicators;
  5. Recommendations;
  6. Whether it was previously identified as a risk (threat or opportunity);
  7. Logged by;
  8. Date raised;
  9. Status: The current status of the lesson and the date of last update;
  10. Priority: In terms of the project's chosen categories;
  11. Action(s): Details of any action taken.

A.14.3 Derivation

- Lessons Reports from other projects;
- Project mandate or Project Brief;
- Daily Log, Issue Register, Quality Register and Risk Register;
- Checkpoint Reports and Highlight Reports;
- Completed Work Packages;
- Stage Plans with actuals;
- Observation and experience of the project's processes.

A.14.4 Format and Presentation

A Lessons Log can take a number of formats, including:

- Document, spreadsheet or database;
- Stand-alone log or a carry forward in progress review minutes.

The Lessons Log may be part of an integrated project register for all risks, actions, decisions, assumptions, Issue Reports, lessons, etc.

A.14.5 Quality Criteria

- The status indicates whether action has been taken.
- Lessons are uniquely identified, including to which product they refer.
- A process is defined using which the Lessons Log is updated.
- Access to the Lessons Log is controlled.
- The Lessons Log is kept in a safe place.

A.15 LESSONS REPORT

A.15.1 Purpose

To pass on any lessons that can be usefully applied to other projects.

The purpose of the report is to provoke action so that the positive lessons become embedded in the organization(s)'s way of working and that the organization(s) is/are able to avoid the negative lessons on future projects.

A Lessons Report should always be part of the End Project Report, but can be raised at any time in a project. A Lessons Report may be included as part of an End Stage Report.

The data in the report should be used by the corporate group that is responsible for the QMS, in order to refine, change and improve the standards. Statistics on how much effort was needed for products can help improve future estimating.

A.15.2 Composition

- Executive summary;
- Scope of the report (e.g. stage or project);
- A review of what went well, what went badly and any recommendations for corporate/programme management consideration; in particular:
  1. Project management method,
  2. Any specialist methods used,
  3. Project strategies (risk management, quality management, communications management and configuration management),
  4. Project controls (and the effectiveness of any tailoring),
  5. Abnormal events causing deviations;
- A review of useful measurements such as:
  1. How much effort was required to create the products,
  2. How effective was the QMS in designing, developing and delivering fit-for-purpose products (e.g. how many errors were found after products had passed quality checks),
  3. Statistics on issues and risks;
- For significant lessons it may be useful to provide additional details on:
  1. Event,
  2. Effect (e.g. positive/negative financial impact),
  3. Causes/trigger,
  4. Whether there were any early warning indicators,
  5. Recommendations,
  6. Whether it was previously identified as a risk (threat or opportunity).

A.15.3 Derivation

- Project Initiation Documentation (for the baselined position);
- Lessons Log;
- Quality Register, Issue Register, Risk Register;
- Communication Management Strategy (for the distribution list).

A.15.4 Format and Presentation

A Lessons Report can take a number of formats, including:

- Verbal report to Project Board (could be in person or by phone);
- Presentation at a progress review (physical meeting or conference call);
- Document or email issued to the Project Board.

A.15.5 Quality Criteria

- Every management control has been examined.
- Statistics of estimates vs. actuals are provided.
- Statistics of the success of quality controls used are included.
- Any appointed Project Assurance roles agree with the report.
- Unexpected risks are reviewed to determine if they could have been anticipated.
- Recommended actions are provided for each lesson (note: lessons are not 'learned' until action is taken).

A.16 PLAN

A.16.1 Purpose

A plan provides a statement of how and when objectives are to be achieved, by showing the major products, activities and resources required for the scope of the plan.

A.16.2 Composition

- Plan Description: A brief description of what the plan covers (i.e. project, stage, team, exception) and the planning approach;

- Plan Prerequisites: Any fundamental aspects which must be in place and remain in place for the plan to succeed;
- External Dependencies: Any external factor that may influence the plan;
- Planning Assumptions: Assumptions on which the plan is based;
- Lessons Incorporated: Details of any relevant lessons from previous similar projects accommodated within this plan;
- Monitoring and Control: How the plan will be monitored and controlled;
- Budgets: Time and cost, including provisions for risks and changes;
- Tolerances: Time, cost and scope tolerances for the level of plan;
- Product Descriptions: For the products of the plan (for the Project Plan this will be the Project Product, for the Stage Plan this will be the Stage Products and for a Team Plan this will be a reference to the relevant Work Package);
- Schedule: Which may include graphical representations of:
  1. Product Breakdown Structure,
  2. Product Flow Diagram,
  3. Activity network,
  4. Gantt or bar chart,
  5. Table of resource requirements,
  6. Table of requested/assigned specific resources.

A.16.3 Derivation

- Project Brief;
- Quality Management Strategy (if any quality management activities are to be included in the plan);
- Risk Management Strategy (any risk management activities to be included in the plan);
- Communication Management Strategy (any communication activities to be included in the plan)
- Configuration Management Strategy (any configuration management activities to be included in the plan)
- Resource availability;
- Registers and Logs.

A.16.4 Format and Presentation

A plan can take a number of formats, including:

- A stand-alone document or a section of the Project Initiation Documentation;
- Document, spreadsheet, presentation slides or mindmap.

A.16.5 Quality Criteria

- The plan is achievable.
- Estimates are based on consultation with the resources who will undertake the work and/or historical data.
- It is planned to an appropriate level of detail.
- The plan conforms to required corporate or programme standards.
- (For Stage and Team Plans) The plan covers management and control activities (such as quality) as well as the activities to create the products in scope.
- The plan supports the management controls defined in the Project Initiation Documentation.

A.17 PRODUCT DESCRIPTION

A.17.1 Purpose

A Product Description is used to:

- Define who the users of the product will be understand the detailed nature, purpose, function and appearance of the product;
- Identify the sources of information or supply for the product;
- Identify the level of quality required of the product;
- Enable identification of activities to produce, review and approve the product;
- Define the people or skills required to produce, review and approve the product.

A.17.2 Composition

- Identifier;
- Title;

- Purpose: This defines the purpose that the product will fulfil;
- Owner: The person or group responsible for the definition of the product and any decision to amend this;
- Composition: This is a list of the parts of the product;
- Derivation: Examples are:
  1. a design is derived from a specification,
  2. a product is brought in from a supplier,
  3. a statement of the expected benefits are obtained from the user,
  4. a product is obtained from another department or team;
- Format and Presentation: Any standard appearance to which the product must conform;
- Development Skills Required: An indication of the skills required to develop the product; identification of the actual people may be left until planning the stage in which the product is to be created;
- Quality Criteria: To what quality specification must the product be produced and what quality measurements will be applied by those inspecting the finished product;
- Quality Method: What kinds of quality method – e.g., design verification, pilot, test, inspection or review – are to be used to check the quality or functionality of the product;
- Quality Tolerance: Details of any range in the quality criteria within which the product would be acceptable;
- Quality Skills Required: An indication of the skills required to undertake quality control; identification of the actual people may be left until planning the stage in which the quality check is to be done;
- Quality Responsibilities: Defining the presenter, reviewer(s) and approver(s) for the product.

A.17.3 Derivation

- Product Breakdown Structure;
- The end users of the product;
- Quality Management Strategy;
- Configuration Management Strategy.

A.17.4 Format and Presentation

A Product Description can take a number of formats, including:

- Document, presentation slides or mindmap.

A.17.5 Quality Criteria

- The purpose is clear and consistent with other products.
- The product is described to a level of detail sufficient to plan and manage its development.
- The Product Description is concise yet sufficient to enable the product to be produced, reviewed and approved.
- Responsibility for the development of the product is clearly identified.
- Responsibility for the development of the product is consistent with the roles and responsibilities described in the project management team organization and the Quality Management Strategy.
- The quality criteria are consistent with the project quality standards, standard checklists and acceptance criteria.
- The quality criteria can be used to determine whether the product is fit for purpose.
- The types of quality check required are able to verify whether the product meets its stated quality criteria.

A.18 PRODUCT STATUS ACCOUNT

A.18.1 Purpose

The Product Status Account provides information about the state of products within defined limits. The limits can vary. For example, the report could cover the entire project, a particular stage or a particular area of the project. It is particularly useful if the Project Manager wishes to confirm the version number and/or status of products.

A.18.2 Composition

- Report Scope: Describing the scope of the report (e.g. for the entire project, by stage, by product type, by supplier, etc.);
- Date produced.

For each product within scope of the report, the report may include:

- Product identifier and name;
- Version;
- Status and date of last status change;
- Product state;
- Owner;
- Location;
- User;
- Producer and date allocated to producer;
- Planned and actual date Product Description baselined;
- Planned and actual date the product was baselined;
- Planned date for next baseline;
- List of related products;
- List of related Issue Reports (including change requests pending and approved) and risks.

A.18.3 Derivation

- Configuration Records.

A.18.4 Format and Presentation

A Product Status Account can take a number of formats, including:

- Document, spreadsheet, report from a database.

A.18.5 Quality Criteria

- The details and dates match those in the Stage Plan.
- The product name is consistent with the Product Breakdown Structure and the name in the Configuration Item Record.

A.19 PROJECT BRIEF

A.19.1 Purpose

A Project Brief is used to provide a full and firm foundation for the initiation of the project.

A.19.2 Composition

- Project Definition: Explaining what the project needs to achieve; should include:
    1. Background,
    2. Project objectives (covering time, cost, quality, scope, risk, benefit, performance goals),
    3. Desired outcomes,
    4. Project scope and exclusions,
    5. Constraints and assumptions,
    6. The user(s) and any other known interested parties,
    7. Interfaces;
- Outline Business Case: Reasons why the project is needed and the business option selected;
- Project Product Description: Including customer quality expectations, user acceptance criteria and operations and maintenance acceptance criteria;
- Project Approach: Defines the choice of solution the project will use to deliver the selected business option;
- Project Management Team Structure: A chart showing who will be involved with the project;
- Role Descriptions: For the project management team and any other key resources identified at this time;
- References: To any associated documents or products.

A.19.3 Derivation

- A project mandate supplied at the start of the project;
- Programme Management: If the project is part of a programme, the Project Brief is likely to be supplied by the programme;

- Discussions with corporate regarding corporate strategy and any policies and standards that apply;
- Discussions with the Project Board and users if the project mandate is incomplete;
- Discussions with the operations and maintenance organization (if applicable);
- Discussions with the (potential) suppliers regarding specialist development lifecycles that could be used;
- Lessons Log.

A.19.4 Format and Presentation

A Project Brief can take a number of formats, including:

- Document or presentation slides.

A.19.5 Quality Criteria

- The Project Brief accurately reflects the project mandate and the requirements of the business and the users.
- The project approach considers a range of solutions such as: Bespoke or off-the-shelf, contracted out or developed in-house, design from new or modified existing product, etc.
- The project approach has been selected which maximizes the chance of achieving overall success for the project.
- The project objectives, project approach and strategies are consistent with the organization's corporate social responsibility directive.

A.20 PROJECT INITIATION DOCUMENTATION

A.20.1 Purpose

The Project Initiation Documentation gives the direction and scope of the project and forms the 'contract' between the Project Manager and the Project Board.

The three primary uses of the Project Initiation Documentation are to:

- Ensure that the project has a sound basis before asking the Project Board to make any major commitment to the project.
- Act as a base document against which the Project Board and the Project Manager can assess progress, issues and ongoing viability questions.
- Provide a single source of reference about the project so that people joining the 'temporary organization' can quickly and easily find out what the project is about and how it is being managed.

The Project Initiation Documentation is a living product in that it should always reflect the current status, plans and controls of the project. It will need to be updated and rebaselined, as necessary, at the end of each stage to reflect the current status of its constituent parts.

The Project Initiation Documentation is the basis against which performance will be assessed when closing the project.

A.20.2 Composition

- Project Definition: Explaining what the project needs to achieve. It should include:
  1. Background,
  2. Project objectives and desired outcomes,
  3. Project scope and exclusions,
  4. Constraints and assumptions,
  5. The user(s) and any other known interested parties,
  6. Interfaces;
- Project approach;
- Business Case;
- Project management team structure: a diagram or chart, showing who will be involved in the management team
- Quality Management Strategy;
- Configuration Management Strategy;
- Risk Management Strategy;

- Communication Management Strategy;
- Project Plan;
- Project Controls: Laying down how control is to be exercised within the project, and the reporting and monitoring mechanisms that will support this; it will include the escalation and exception processes;
- A summary of how PRINCE2 will be tailored for the project.

A.20.3 Derivation

- Project Brief;
- Discussions with Business, User and Supplier stakeholders for input on methods, standards and controls.

A.20.4 Format and Presentation

The Project Initiation Documentation could be:

- A single document;
- An index for a collection of documents;
- A document with cross-references to a number of other documents.

A.20.5 Quality Criteria

- The Project Initiation Documentation correctly represents the project.
- It shows a viable, achievable project that is in line with corporate strategy or overall programme needs.
- The project organization structure is complete, with names and titles. All the roles have been considered and are backed up by agreed Role Descriptions. The relationships and lines of authority are clear.
- It clearly shows a control, reporting and direction regime that can be implemented appropriate to the scale, risk and importance of the project to corporate or programme management.
- The controls cover the needs of the Project Board, the Project Manager and the Team Managers and satisfy any delegated assurance requirements.

- It is clear who will administer each control.
- The project objectives, project approach and strategies are consistent with the organization's corporate social responsibility directive and the project controls are adequate to ensure that the project remains compliant with such directive.
- Consideration has been given to the format of the Project Initiation Documentation. For small projects a single document is appropriate. For large projects it may be more appropriate for the Project Initiation Documentation to be a collection of stand-alone documents.

A.21 PROJECT PRODUCT DESCRIPTION

A.21.1 Purpose

The Project Product Description is a special form of Product Description that defines what the project must deliver in order to gain customer acceptance. It is used to:

- Gain agreement from the user on the project's scope and requirements;
- Define the customer's quality expectations;
- Define the acceptance criteria, method and responsibilities for the project.

A.21.2 Composition

- Title;
- Purpose: This defines the purpose that the Project Product will fulfil and who will use it;
- Composition: A description of the major products to be delivered by the project;
- Derivation: Examples are:
    1. Existing products to be modified,
    2. Design specifications,
    3. A feasibility report;

- Development Skills Required: An indication of the skills required to develop the product;
- Customer's Quality Expectations;
- Acceptance Criteria: Measurable definitions of the attributes that must apply to the set of products to be acceptable to key stakeholders; examples are: ease of use, ease of support, ease of maintenance, appearance, major functions, development costs, running costs, capacity, availability, reliability, security, accuracy, performance;
- Acceptance Method: The means by which acceptance will be confirmed;
- Acceptance Responsibilities: Defining who will be responsible for confirming acceptance.

A.21.3 Derivation

- Project mandate;
- Discussions with the Senior User and Executive.

A.21.4 Format and Presentation

A Product Description for the Project Product can take a number of formats, including:

- Document, presentation slides or mindmap.

A.21.5 Quality Criteria

- The purpose is clear.
- The composition defines the complete scope of the project.
- The Acceptance Criteria form the complete list against which the project will be assessed.
- The Acceptance Criteria address the requirements of all the key stakeholders (e.g. operations and maintenance).
- It defines how the users and the operational and maintenance organizations will assess the acceptability of the finished product(s).

- All criteria are measurable.
- Each criterion is individually realistic.
- The criteria are realistic and consistent as a set. For example, high quality, early delivery and low cost may not go together.
- The quality expectations have been considered.
- The characteristics of the key quality requirements (e.g. fast/slow, large/small, national/global).
- The elements of the customer QMS that should be used.
- Any other standards that should be used.

A.22 QUALITY MANAGEMENT STRATEGY

A.22.1 Purpose

A Quality Management Strategy is used to define the quality techniques and standards to be applied, and the various responsibilities for achieving the required quality levels during the project.

A.22.2 Composition

- Introduction: It states the purpose, objectives, scope and owner of the strategy.
- Quality Management Procedure: It is a description of (or reference to) the quality management procedure to be used. Any variance from corporate or programme management quality standards should be highlighted, together with a justification for the variance. The procedure should cover:
1. Quality Planning;
2. Quality Control: The project's approach to quality control activities; this may include:
   - Quality Standards,
   - Templates and forms to be employed (e.g. Product Descriptions, Quality Register),
   - Definitions of types of quality checking activities (e.g. inspection, pilot),

- Metrics to be employed in support of quality control.
3. Quality Assurance: It is the project's approach to quality assurance activities. This may include:
    - Responsibilities of the Project Board,
    - Compliance audits,
    - Corporate or programme management reviews.
4. Tools and Techniques: It refers to any QMSs or tools to be used and any preference for techniques which may be used for each step in the Quality Management procedure.
5. Records: They have the definition of what quality records will be required and where they will be stored.
6. Reporting: It describes any quality management reports that are to be produced, their purpose, timing and recipients.
7. Timing of Quality Management Activities: It states when formal quality management activities are to be undertaken, e.g. audits (this may be a reference to the Quality Register).
8. Roles and Responsibilities: It defines the roles and responsibilities of the project team with respect to quality management activities including those with quality responsibilities from corporate or programme management.

A.22.3 Derivation

- Project Board;
- Project Brief;
- Project management team structure (for roles and responsibilities);
- Project Product Description (for customer's quality expectations and acceptance criteria);
- Organizational standards;
- Supplier and customer QMSs;
- Configuration management requirements;
- Change control requirements;
- Corporate or programme strategies;
- Facilitated workshops and informal discussions.

A.22.4 Format and Presentation

A Quality Management Strategy can take a number of formats, including:

- Stand-alone document;
- A section of the Project Initiation Documentation.

A.22.5 Quality Criteria

- The strategy clearly defines ways in which the customer's quality expectations will be met.
- Those defined ways are sufficient to achieve the required quality.
- Responsibilities for quality are defined to a level that is independent of the project and the Project Manager.
- The strategy conforms to the corporate or programme quality policy.
- The approaches to assuring quality for the project are appropriate in light of the standards selected.

A.23 QUALITY REGISTER

A.23.1 Purpose

A Quality Register is used to summarize all the quality management activities that are planned/have taken place. Its purpose is to:

- Provide a unique reference for each quality check;
- Act as a pointer to the quality check documentation for a product;
- Act as a summary of the number and type of quality checks held.

A.23.2 Composition

For each entry in the Quality Register, the following should be recorded:

- Quality Identifier: It provides a unique reference for every quality management activity entered into the Quality Register.
- Product Identifier(s): It is the unique identifier for the product(s) to which the quality management activity relates.

- Product Name: It is the name by which the product is called.
- Roles and Responsibilities: They are the person or team responsible for the quality check, e.g. the Presenter, the Reviewer(s), the Chair.
- Dates: These are planned, forecast and actual dates for:
  1. The quality check;
  2. Sign-off that the quality check is complete.
- Method: It is the method employed for the quality check (e.g. pilot, quality review, audit, etc.).
- Quality Check Documentation: It refers to the quality check documentation for a product, e.g. a test plan.
- Quality Records: It refers to the quality inspection documentation such as the details of any actions required to correct errors and omissions of the products being inspected.
- Result: It is the result of the quality management activity.
- Error Statistics: These provide the number of errors or omissions in the product.

A.23.3 Derivation

- Entries are made when a quality check is entered on a Stage Plan. It may be updated when a Team Plan is created.
- The remaining information comes from the actual performance of the quality check.
- The sign-off date is when all corrective actions have been signed off.

A.23.4 Format and Presentation

A Quality Register can take a number of formats, including:

- Document, spreadsheet or database.

A.23.5 Quality Criteria

- A procedure is in place that will ensure that every quality check is entered on the Quality Register.
- Responsibility for the Quality Register has been allocated.

- The quality method is described in the Quality Management Strategy.
- Actions are clearly described and have owners.
- Entries are uniquely identified, including to which product they refer.
- Access to the Quality Register is controlled.
- The Quality Register is kept in a safe place.
- All quality checks are at an appropriate level of control.

A.24 RISK MANAGEMENT STRATEGY

A.24.1 Purpose

A Risk Management Strategy describes the specific risk management techniques and standards to be applied and the responsibilities for achieving an effective risk management procedure.

A.24.2 Composition

- Introduction: The purpose, objectives, scope and owner of the strategy.
- The Risk Management Procedure: The procedure should cover the risk steps:
  1. Identify (Identify Context and Identify Risks);
  2. Assess (Estimate and Evaluate);
  3. Plan;
  4. Implement;
  5. Communicate.
- Tools and Techniques: Any risk management systems, tools and techniques which may be used for each step in the risk management procedure.
- Records: Definition of what risk records will be required and where they will be stored.
- Reporting: Any risk management reports that are to be produced, their purpose, timing and recipients.

- Timing of risk management activities: When formal risk management activities are to be undertaken; e.g., at End-stage Assessments.
- Roles and Responsibilities: The roles and responsibilities of the project team with respect to risk management activities.
- Scales: The scales for estimating probability and impact for the project to ensure that these are relevant to the cost and time-frame of the project.
- Proximity: Guidance on how proximity for risk events is to be assessed.
- Risk Categories: The risk categories to be used (if at all).
- Risk Response Categories: The risk response categories to be used.
- Early Warning Indicators: Any indicators to be used to track critical aspects of the project so that if certain predefined levels are reached, corrective action will be triggered.
- Risk Tolerance: Defining the threshold levels of risk exposure, which when exceeded requires the risk to be escalated to the next level of management. The risk tolerance should define the risk expectations of corporate or programme management and the Project Board.
- Risk budget: explaining if a risk budget is to be given and, if so, how it is to be used.

A.24.3 Derivation

- Project Brief;
- Business Case;
- The organization's Risk Management Process Guide;
- Programme Risk Management Strategy.

A.24.4 Format and Presentation

A Risk Management Strategy can take a number of formats, including:

- Stand-alone document;
- A section of the Project Initiation Documentation.

A.24.5 Quality Criteria

- Responsibilities are clear and understood by both the customer and the supplier.
- The risk management procedure is clearly documented and can be understood by all parties.
- Scales, expected value and proximity definitions are clear and unambiguous.
- The chosen scales are appropriate for the level of control required.
- Risk reporting requirements are fully defined.

A.25 RISK REGISTER

A.25.1 Purpose

A Risk Register provides a record of identified risks. It is used to capture and maintain information on all of the identified threats and opportunities relating to the project.

A.25.2 Composition

For each entry in the Risk Register, the following should be recorded:

- Risk Identifier;
- Risk Author;
- Date Registered;
- Risk Category: Schedule, quality, legal, etc.;
- Risk Description: In terms of the cause, event (threat or opportunity);
- Probability, Impact and Expected Value: It is helpful to estimate the *inherent* values (preresponse action) and *residual* values (post-response action);
- Proximity: How close to the present time the risk event is anticipated to happen (e.g. imminent, within stage, within project, beyond project);
- Risk Response Categories:
  1. For threats: Avoid, reduce, fall-back, transfer, accept, share,
  2. For opportunities: Enhance, exploit, reject, share;

- Risk Response: Actions to resolve the risk (should be aligned to the chosen response categories; note, more than one risk response may apply to a risk);
- Risk Status: Typically described in terms of whether the risk is active or closed;
- Risk Owner: The person responsible for managing the risk (there can be only one risk owner per risk);
- Risk Actionee: The person(s) who will implement the action(s) described in the risk response. This may or may not be the same person as the risk owner.

A.25.3 Derivation

- The composition, format and presentation of the Risk Register will be derived from the Risk Management Strategy.
- Entries are made on the Risk Register once a new risk has been identified.
- Daily Log – often issues raised to the Project Manager and captured in the Daily Log are actually risks and only identified as such after further examination.

A.25.4 Format and Presentation

A Risk Register can take a number of formats, including:

- Document, spreadsheet or database;
- The Risk Register may be part of an integrated project register for all risks, actions, decisions, assumptions, Issue Reports, lessons, etc.

A.25.5 Quality Criteria

- The status indicates whether action has been taken.
- Risks are uniquely identified, including to which product they refer.
- Access to the Risk Register is controlled and it is kept in a safe place.

A.26 WORK PACKAGE

A.26.1 Purpose

A Work Package is a set of information about one or more required products collated by the Project Manager to pass responsibility for work to a Team Manager or team member.

A.26.2 Composition

Although the content may vary greatly according to the relationship between the Project Manager and the recipient of the Work Package, it should cover:

- Date;
- Team or person authorized;
- Work Package Description: A description of the work to be done;
- Specialist techniques, processes and procedures: Not including PRINCE2 processes;
- Development Interfaces: Interfaces that must be maintained while developing the products; these may be people providing information or those who need to receive information;
- Operations and Maintenance Interfaces: Identification of any specialist products with which the products in the Work Package will have to interface during their operational life;
- Configuration Management Requirements: Any arrangements that must be made by the producer for version control of the products in the Work Package, obtaining copies of other products or their Product Descriptions, submission of the product to configuration management, any storage or security requirements and any need to advise Project Support of changes in the status of the Work Package;
- Joint Agreements: Details of the agreements on effort, cost, start and end dates, and tolerances for the Work Package (the tolerances will be for time and cost but may also include scope and risk);
- Constraints: Any constraints (apart from the tolerances) on the work, people to be involved, timings, charges, rules to be followed (e.g. security and safety), etc.;

- Reporting Arrangements: The expected frequency and content of Checkpoint Reports;
- Problem Handling and Escalation: This refers to the procedure for raising issues and risks;
- Extracts or references: Any extracts or references to related documents, specifically:
  1. Stage Plan Extract: This will be the relevant section of the Stage Plan;
  2. Product Description(s): An attachment of the Product Description(s) for the products identified in the Work Package;
  3. Approval Requirements: The person, role or group who will approve the completed Work Package and how the Project Manager is to be advised of completion of the Work Package.

There should be space on the Work Package to record its authorization and acceptance of the return of the completed Work Package. This can be enhanced to include an assessment of the work and go towards performance appraisal.

A.26.3 Derivation

- Existing commercial agreements between customer and supplier (if any);
- Quality Management Strategy;
- Configuration Management Strategy;
- Stage Plan.

A.26.4 Format and Presentation

A Work Package can take a number of formats, including:

- Document;
- Verbal conversation between the Project Manager and a Team Manager.

The Work Package will vary in content and in degree of formality depending on circumstances.

Where the work is being carried out by a supplier under a contract, there is a need for a formal written instruction in line with standards laid down in that contract.

A.26.5 Quality Criteria

- The required Work Package is clearly defined and understood by the assigned resource.
- There is a Product Description for the required product(s), with clearly identified and acceptable quality criteria.
- The Product Description matches up with the other Work Package documentation.
- Standards for the work are agreed upon.
- All necessary interfaces have been defined.
- The reporting arrangements include the provision for exception reporting.
- There is agreement between the Project Manager and the recipient on the Work Package.
- The dates and effort are in line with those shown in the Stage Plan for the current management stage.
- Reporting arrangements are defined.
- Any requirement for independent attendance at, and participation in, quality checking is defined.

PRINCE2 Foundation Exam

B.1 GENERAL

The Foundation exam is one-hour long, and is 'closed book', which means you may not have access to any books during the exam.

There will be 75 multi-choice questions in the Foundation exam. Marks scored in 70 of these will count towards the exam score. The other five are trials of questions as part of 'quality review' before they are actually used as bona fide exam questions. Candidate answers to the questions are reviewed to see if they are understood, acceptable and answered correctly by a certain percentage of candidates. Candidates need to score at least 50%, which is 35 out of the 70 genuine questions. Candidates do not know which are the five questions being trialled.

All questions are of the classic type: a question, followed by four options, of which one only is correct. There are four styles of questions:

- Standard: A simple question, four options of which one and only one is the correct answer.
- Negative: A question of what is NOT or what is FALSE. The answer will be one of the four options offered, which means that the other three will be TRUE.
- Missing word: The question is presented as a statement where one or more words are replaced by [?]. The candidate has to select the missing word or words from the four options.

- List: The question will be a statement with four bullet points. The candidate has to select the three bullet points that fit the statement. In other words, this is similar to the Negative style, with three correct and only one incorrect bullet.

Questions can be at Learning Level 1 or Learning Level 2. Learning Level 1 questions test knowledge and use the words from the manual (or in this case, this book), e.g. 'Do you remember reading this?'. Learning Level 2 questions test comprehension and do not use the same wording as the manual, i.e. 'Do you understand the principles and concepts? Can you understand how they are used?'

In the next few pages there is a sample paper for you to test your PRINCE2 knowledge and understanding. Following that there is an answer sheet for you to write down your answers. I recommend that you copy and use the blank answer sheet, rather than write on the questions themselves. This way you can retake the exam at any time to test your improving knowledge. After the blank answer sheet, you will find each question repeated, but this time with the correct answer shown, a reference to where in the book you can find the answer and a description of why each option is either correct or wrong.

B.2 STYLE EXAMPLES

Below are a few examples of each style of question.

B.2.1 Standard

E1. Which is a PRINCE2 Principle?   Tick one of these boxes

    a) Learn from experience   ☐
    a) Plans   ☐
    b) Controls   ☐
    c) Define the quality   ☐

E2. Which theme discusses the importance of knowing why a project should be undertaken?   Tick one of these boxes

    a) Risk   ☐
    b) Quality   ☐

Tick one of these boxes

c) Business Case ☐
d) Change ☐

B.2.2 Negative

E3. Which of the following is NOT   Tick one of these boxes
a PRINCE2 benefit?

a) Explicitly recognizes project ☐
responsibilities
b) Ensures that participants focus ☐
on the viability of the project
c) Defines a thorough but ☐
economical structure of reports
d) Avoids involving stakeholders ☐
who are merely interested
parties

E4. Which is NOT an aspect of project   Tick one of these boxes
performance to be managed?

a) Costs ☐
b) Timescales ☐
c) Benefits ☐
d) Delegation ☐

B.2.3 Missing Word

E5. Fill in the missing words in the   Tick one of these boxes
following sentence.

The PRINCE2 processes address
the [?] of the project.

a) shape and size ☐
b) chronological flow ☐
c) reasons and benefits ☐
d) planning and reporting ☐

E6. Fill in the missing words in the   Tick one of these boxes
      following sentence.

      PRINCE2 defines a project as a [?]
      that is created for the purpose of
      delivering business products.

      a) specialist stage   ☐
      b) temporary organization   ☐
      c) fixed set of resources   ☐
      d) set of mandatory techniques   ☐

B.2.4 List

E7. Which of the following are   Tick one of these boxes
      PRINCE2 plans?

      1. Exception Plan
      2. Stage Plan
      3. Quality Plan
      4. Benefits Review Plan

          a) 1, 2, 3   ☐
          b) 1, 2, 4   ☐
          c) 1, 3, 4   ☐
          d) 2, 3, 4   ☐

E8. Which of the following are risk   Tick one of these boxes
      responses?

      1. Avoid
      2. Enhance
      3. Fallback
      4. Ignore

          a) 1, 2, 3   ☐
          b) 1, 2, 4   ☐
          c) 1, 3, 4   ☐
          d) 2, 3, 4   ☐

B.3 SAMPLE FOUNDATION EXAM PAPER

1.   Which is a PRINCE2 Principle?   Tick one of these boxes

     a) Learn from experience   ☐
     b) Plans   ☐
     c) Controls   ☐
     d) Define the quality   ☐

2.   Which theme discusses the importance of knowing why a project should be undertaken?

     a) Risk   ☐
     b) Quality   ☐
     c) Business Case   ☐
     d) Plans   ☐

3.   Which of the following is NOT a PRINCE2 benefit?

     a) Clearly identifies project responsibilities   ☐
     b) Ensures that participants focus on the viability of the project   ☐
     c) Defines a thorough but economical structure of reports   ☐
     d) Avoids involving stakeholders who are merely interested parties   ☐

4.   Which is NOT an aspect of project performance to be managed?

     a) Costs   ☐
     b) Timescales   ☐
     c) Benefits   ☐
     d) Delegation   ☐

5. Fill in the missing words in the   Tick one of these boxes
    following sentence.

    The PRINCE2 processes address the
    [?] of the project.

    a) shape and size   ☐
    b) chronological flow   ☐
    c) quality assurance   ☐
    d) planning and reporting   ☐

6. Fill in the missing words in the
    following sentence.

    PRINCE2 defines a project as a [?]
    that is created for the purpose of
    delivering business products.

    a) specialist stage   ☐
    b) temporary organization   ☐
    c) fixed set of resources   ☐
    d) set of mandatory techniques   ☐

7. Which of the following are
    PRINCE2 plans?

    1. Exception Plan
    2. Stage Plan
    3. Quality Plan
    4. Benefits Review Plan
         a) 1, 2, 3   ☐
         b) 1, 2, 4   ☐
         c) 1, 3, 4   ☐
         d) 2, 3, 4   ☐

8. Which of the following are risk
    responses?

    1. Avoid
    2. Enhance

3. Fallback   Tick one of these boxes
4. Ignore
    a) 1, 2, 3   ☐
    b) 1, 2, 4   ☐
    c) 1, 3, 4   ☐
    d) 2, 3, 4   ☐

9.   Before the Risk Register is created where will the Project Manager record any risks?

    a) Quality Register   ☐
    b) Daily Log   ☐
    c) Issue Register   ☐
    d) Lessons Log   ☐

10.   What is the trigger for a project?

    a) Project Initiation   ☐
       Documentation
    b) Project Brief   ☐
    c) Business Case   ☐
    d) Project Mandate   ☐

11.   In which process is the request for project funding defined in detail?

    a) Starting up a Project   ☐
    b) Initiating a Project   ☐
    c) Directing a Project   ☐
    d) Closing a Project   ☐

12.   Which activities are carried out by the role of the quality review chair?

    1. Check that the product is ready for review.

   2. Gather all question lists and set   Tick one of these boxes
     the review meeting agenda.
   3. Lead the review team through
     the product section by section.
   4. Ensure that all agreed errors are
     recorded on a follow-up action
     list.
     a) 1, 2, 3 ☐
     b) 1, 2, 4 ☐
     c) 1, 3, 4 ☐
     d) 2, 3, 4 ☐

13. Which does NOT involve the Project Board?

a) Exception assessment ☐
b) Highlight Reports ☐
c) Work Package authorization ☐
d) Project closure ☐

14. Identify the missing words in the following sentence.

Effective risk management is a prerequisite of the [?] Principle.
a) focus on products ☐
b) continued business justification ☐
c) manage by exception ☐
d) manage by stages ☐

15. How are Principles characterized?

a) Are capable of tailoring ☐
b) Justify the project ☐
c) Apply to every project ☐
d) Their use is optional ☐

16. Which is independent of the project management team?

Tick one of these boxes

 a) Team Manager ☐
 b) Project Assurance ☐
 c) Project Support ☐
 d) Quality Assurance ☐

17. Which product defines the authorities for handling requests for change?

 a) Communication Management
    Strategy ☐
 b) Configuration Management
    Strategy ☐
 c) Quality Management Strategy ☐
 d) Risk Management Strategy ☐

18. Which are basic business options?

 1. Do nothing
 2. Do less
 3. Do something
 4. Do the minimum
    a) 1, 2, 3 ☐
    b) 1, 2, 4 ☐
    c) 1, 3, 4 ☐
    d) 2, 3, 4 ☐

19. Which part of the Business Case balances costs against benefits over a period of time?

 a) Expected benefits ☐
 b) Business options ☐
 c) Investment appraisal ☐
 d) Expected disbenefits ☐

20. Which role is responsible for   Tick one of these boxes
    realizing post-project benefits?

    a) Executive   ☐
    b) Senior User   ☐
    c) Senior Supplier   ☐
    d) Project Manager   ☐

21. Which of the following statements
    is FALSE?

    a) A company's quality management   ☐
       system becomes part of PRINCE2.
    b) Customer's quality expectations   ☐
       should be discovered in the
       Starting up a Project process.
    c) PRINCE2 may form part of a   ☐
       company's quality management
       system.
    d) The use of Team Plans is optional.   ☐

22. Which is NOT one of the four tasks
    of the Product-based Planning
    technique?

    a) Identifying dependencies   ☐
    b) Producing a Product Breakdown   ☐
       Structure
    c) Creating a Product Checklist   ☐
    d) Writing Product Descriptions of   ☐
       each significant product

23. Which of the following reviews the
    benefits achieved by the project?

    a) End Project Report   ☐
    b) Lessons Report   ☐
    c) Post-project benefits review   ☐
    d) Quality review   ☐

24. Who is responsible for assessing and updating the Business Case at the end of a stage?   Tick one of these boxes
   a) Senior User ☐
   b) Executive ☐
   c) Project Manager ☐
   d) Project Assurance ☐

25. Whose role is it to ensure that planned communications actually occur?
   a) Project Board ☐
   b) Project Manager ☐
   c) Project Assurance ☐
   d) Corporate management ☐

26. In which process is the Project Quality Strategy (QMS) created?
   a) Starting up a Project ☐
   b) Initiating a Project ☐
   c) Directing a Project ☐
   d) Managing a Stage Boundary ☐

27. Which theme is central to the approach to quality?
   a) Manage by exception ☐
   b) Continued business justification ☐
   c) Focus on products ☐
   d) Defined roles and responsibilities ☐

28. Which product relates planned quality activities to those actually performed?
   a) Quality Register ☐
   b) Project Approach ☐

Tick one of these boxes

c) Quality Management Strategy   ☐
d) Lessons Log   ☐

29. Which action is NOT part of
    Accept a Work Package?

    a) Agree upon tolerance margins.   ☐
    b) Understand the reporting   ☐
       requirements.
    c) Produce a Team Plan.   ☐
    d) Monitor and control any Work   ☐
       Package risks.

30. Comparing a product against defined
    criteria is an objective of what?

    a) Work Package   ☐
    b) Investment appraisal   ☐
    c) Quality review   ☐
    d) Quality Register   ☐

31. Which process defines Quality
    responsibilities?

    a) Starting up a Project   ☐
    b) Initiating a Project   ☐
    c) Directing a Project   ☐
    d) Managing a Stage Boundary   ☐

32. Whose responsibility is it to check
    that a product is ready for its
    quality review?

    a) Chair   ☐
    b) Administrator   ☐
    c) Presenter   ☐
    d) Reviewer   ☐

33. Whose task is it to produce products consistent with their Product Descriptions?

a) Senior User ☐
b) Project Manager ☐
c) Team Manager ☐
d) Senior Supplier ☐

34. What provides the Business Case with planned costs?

a) Project Brief ☐
b) Project Plan ☐
c) Initiation Stage Plan ☐
d) Project Approach ☐

35. What is identified first in the PRINCE2 planning philosophy?

a) Dependencies ☐
b) Activities ☐
c) Products ☐
d) Resources ☐

36. In which process is the means of reviewing benefits developed?

a) Closing a Project ☐
b) Initiating a Project ☐
c) Managing a Stage Boundary ☐
d) Starting up a Project ☐

37. In which process are previous lessons captured?

a) Starting up a Project ☐
b) Initiating a Project ☐
c) Managing a Stage Boundary ☐
d) Closing a Project ☐

38. Which product defines whether
the solution will be developed
in-house?

Tick one of these boxes

a) Project mandate ☐
b) Project approach ☐
c) Business Case ☐
d) Project Plan ☐

39. Which process ensures that there
is an interface with corporate
management throughout the
project?

a) Starting up a Project ☐
b) Managing a Stage Boundary ☐
c) Directing a Project ☐
d) Initiating a Project ☐

40. Which statement is NOT a purpose
of the *Closing a Project* process?

a) Confirm acceptance by the
customer of the project's
products. ☐
b) Recognize that the project has
nothing more to contribute. ☐
c) Recognize that approved
changes to the objectives in the
Project Initiation Document
have been achieved. ☐
d) Place formal requirements on
accepting and delivering project
work. ☐

41. Which is NOT a Project Board
activity?

a) Authorize initiation ☐
b) Give ad hoc direction ☐

Tick one of these boxes

c) Authorize a Work Package ☐
d) Authorize the project ☐

42. What information is the trigger for the *Starting up a Project* process?

a) Project mandate ☐
b) Project Initiation Document ☐
c) An appointed Executive ☐
d) Outline Business Case ☐

43. Which of the following is NOT input to the Project Board?

a) Informal request for advice ☐
b) Escalated Issue Report ☐
c) Project authorization notification ☐
d) Highlight Report ☐

44. Which document contains any follow-on action recommendations?

a) Lessons Report ☐
b) End Stage Report ☐
c) End Project Report ☐
d) Benefits Review Plan ☐

45. Which product captures user quality expectations and acceptance criteria?

a) Project Product Description ☐
b) Quality Management Strategy ☐
c) Project Brief ☐
d) Daily Log ☐

46. Which of the following are done in   Tick one of these boxes
    the *Starting up a Project* process?

    1) Set up the project management
       team.
    2) Develop the project mandate
       into the Project Brief.
    3) Create the Issue Register.
    4) Devise the project approach.
       a) 1, 2, 3   ☐
       b) 1, 2, 4   ☐
       c) 1, 3, 4   ☐
       d) 2, 3, 4   ☐

47. An example of Work Package [?]
    might be 'I need this by Thursday
    close of work, but by Friday
    lunchtime at the latest'.

    a) Approval requirements   ☐
    b) Constraints   ☐
    c) Tolerance   ☐
    d) Reporting and problem handling   ☐

48. Configuration management is
    described in which theme?

    a) Quality   ☐
    b) Plans   ☐
    c) Progress   ☐
    d) Change   ☐

49. Which are purposes of a summary
    risk profile?

    1. Shows the risk owners
    2. Snapshot of the risk
       environment

3. Shows risk trends

4. Identifies risks beyond the risk
appetite

Tick one of these boxes

a) 1, 2, 3 □

b) 1, 2, 4 □

c) 1, 3, 4 □

d) 2, 3, 4 □

50. In which process is the Business
Case reviewed and updated?

a) Controlling a Stage □

b) Managing Product Delivery □

c) Managing a Stage Boundary □

d) Directing a Project □

51. Which is NOT part of an
unambiguous expression of a risk?

a) Probability □

b) Cause □

c) Effect □

d) Event □

52. What does an early warning
indicator record?

a) Proximity of a risk. □

b) A project objective could be at
risk. □

c) A note to the Project Board
advising it of a forthcoming
deviation beyond tolerance. □

d) Date of a stage end is
approaching. □

53. What does a risk budget cover?

a) Cost of risks carried
over to follow-on action
recommendations □

Tick one of these boxes

b) Off-specification costs ☐
c) Costs of administering risk ☐
   management
d) Cost of fallback plans ☐

54. Which document contains
    the Issue and Change Control
    procedure?

a) Quality Management Strategy ☐
b) Configuration Management ☐
   Strategy
c) Risk Management Strategy ☐
d) Communication Management ☐
   Strategy

55. What is product status accounting?

a) Recording Work Package ☐
   progress from a review of
   timesheets and the Team Plan
b) An audit comparing actual ☐
   product status with that shown
   in the Configuration Item
   Records
c) Reporting on the current and ☐
   historical state of products
d) A summary of the state of the ☐
   Quality Register at the end of a
   stage

56. What is the second step in an Issue
    and Change Control procedure?

a) Decide ☐
b) Capture ☐
c) Propose ☐
d) Examine ☐

57. Which Principle is NOT supported   Tick one of these boxes
    by the Progress theme?

    a) Manage by exception   ☐
    b) Continued business justification   ☐
    c) Tailoring PRINCE2   ☐
    d) Manage by stages   ☐

58. Who sets project tolerances?

    a) Corporate Management   ☐
    b) Project Board   ☐
    c) Project Manager   ☐
    d) Executive   ☐

59. Why might dividing a project into
    a small number of lengthy stages
    be a problem?

    a) Makes project planning more   ☐
       difficult
    b) Increases project management   ☐
       administration costs
    c) Reduces the level of Project   ☐
       Board control
    d) Reduces the amount of risk   ☐
       monitoring

60. Which is an event-driven control?

    a) Highlight Report   ☐
    b) Checkpoint Report   ☐
    c) End Stage Report   ☐
    d) Review Work Package status   ☐

61. Which product is NOT reviewed
    when reviewing Work Package
    status?

    a) Checkpoint Report   ☐
    b) Project Plan   ☐

Tick one of these boxes

    c) Team Plan ☐
    d) Quality Register ☐

62. Where are suitable reviewers first identified for a quality review?

    a) Quality Management Strategy ☐
    b) Project Plan ☐
    c) Quality review preparation step ☐
    d) Stage Plan ☐

63. Which of the following statements are TRUE?

    1) The Executive is responsible for the business interests of the customer and supplier.
    2) There will always be two Business Cases in customer/ supplier situations.
    3) The customer and supplier may be part of the same corporate body, or may be independent of each other.
    4) A project's Business Case means the customer's Business Case.
        a) 1, 2, 3 ☐
        b) 1, 2, 4 ☐
        c) 1, 3, 4 ☐
        d) 2, 3, 4 ☐

64. Which product reviews a project's actual achievements against the Project Initiation Document?

    a) Lessons Report ☐
    b) Follow-on action recommendations ☐

Tick one of these boxes

   c) End Project Report ☐
   d) Benefits Review Plan ☐

65. Which product records a forecast failure to meet a requirement?

   a) Risk Register ☐
   b) Concession ☐
   c) Highlight Report ☐
   d) Off-specification ☐

66. What product would the Project Manager call for when reviewing stage status to check on a phased hand-over of products?

   a) Stage Plan ☐
   b) Quality Register ☐
   c) Product Status Account ☐
   d) Risk Register ☐

67. Who should prepare the outline Business Case?

   a) Senior User ☐
   b) Executive ☐
   c) Project Manager ☐
   d) Corporate Management ☐

68. If an issue can be dealt with informally, where should a note of it be made?

   a) Issue Register ☐
   b) Daily Log ☐
   c) Lessons Log ☐
   d) Risk Register ☐

69. Which of these statements is FALSE?   Tick one of these boxes

   a) The Project Board approves   ☐
      Team Plans.
   b) The Project Board approves a   ☐
      stage Exception Plan.
   c) A Stage Plan is required for each   ☐
      stage in the Project Plan.
   d) The Project Plan is an overview   ☐
      of the total project.

70. When would an Exception Report
    be required?

   a) Whenever a new risk is identified.   ☐
   b) When a stakeholder raises a   ☐
      complaint.
   c) When a request for change or   ☐
      off-specification is received.
   d) When a stage is forecast to   ☐
      deviate outside its tolerance
      bounds.

71. What is the final step in risk
    management?

   a) Appoint a risk owner   ☐
   b) Decide   ☐
   c) Communicate   ☐
   d) Implement   ☐

72. When tailoring PRINCE2 for a
    project, which Principles can be
    omitted?

   a) None   ☐
   b) All except continued business   ☐
      justification

Tick one of these boxes

   c) Manage by stages   ☐

   d) Manage by exception   ☐

73. In tailoring a project within a programme environment, why might responsibility for the Benefits Review Plan be removed from the Executive's role?

   a) It might be given to the Senior User   ☐

   b) There may be no project benefits to be reviewed   ☐

   c) It could be moved to Project Assurance   ☐

   d) It becomes a programme responsibility   ☐

74. Which project role would sit on the programme board?

   a) None   ☐

   b) Senior Supplier   ☐

   c) Executive   ☐

   d) Quality assurance   ☐

75. Which theme is most affected when used in simple projects?

   a) Business Case   ☐

   b) Organization   ☐

   c) Risk   ☐

   d) Change   ☐

ANSWER SHEET

Question	Answer	R/W	Question	Answer	R/W	Question	Answer	R/W
1			26			51		
2			27			52		
3			28			53		
4			29			54		
5			30			55		
6			31			56		
7			32			57		
8			33			58		
9			34			59		
10			35			60		
11			36			61		
12			37			62		
13			38			63		
14			39			64		
15			40			65		
16			41			66		
17			42			67		
18			43			68		
19			44			69		
20			45			70		
21			46			71		
22			47			72		
23			48			73		
24			49			74		
25			50			75		

1.   Which is a PRINCE2   Correct Answer:
    Principle?

    a) Learn from experience   ☑
    b) Plans   ☐
    c) Controls   ☐
    d) Define the quality   ☐

    Where to find the answer: 2.3

a) Rationale	Correct. This is the second PRINCE2 Principle, leading to a review of previous projects' Lessons Reports when starting up a project. Any useful lessons are documented in the current project's Lessons Log, which is checked for relevant lessons when creating the products in *Starting up a Project* and *Initiating a Project*.
b) Rationale	No, every project needs plans, so it is not a unique PRINCE2 Principle. It is a theme.
c) Rationale	Not a Principle. Principles are unique to PRINCE2, whereas control is required with any method. Control needs are described in the Progress theme.
d) Rationale	This is just a statement, not a Principle. Quality comes under the 'focus on products' Principle. Quality is a theme.

2. Which theme discusses   Correct Answer:
    the importance of knowing
    why a project should be
    undertaken?

    a) Risk   ☐
    b) Quality   ☐
    c) Business Case   ☑
    d) Plans   ☐

    Where to find the answer: 10.1

    a) Rationale   Risk is to control uncertainty in
                           the execution of a project. The
                           Business Case summarizes the
                           major risks, but this is separate
                           to the reasons for undertaking
                           the project.

    b) Rationale   Quality is not interested in
                           why, just the quality of what is
                           produced.

    c) Rationale   Correct. The Business Case
                           must contain the reasons for
                           undertaking the project.

    d) Rationale   No, plans define how and
                           when you will do something,
                           not why you are doing it.

3. Which of the following is   Correct Answer:
    NOT a PRINCE2 benefit?

    a) Clearly identifies project   ☐
       responsibilities
    b) Ensures that participants   ☐
       focus on the viability of
       the project
    c) Defines a thorough but   ☐
       economical structure of
       reports

d) Avoids involving
   stakeholders who are
   merely interested parties   ☑

Where to find the answer: 1.1

a) Rationale   The Organization theme
explains role responsibilities.

b) Rationale   The Business Case contains the
driving force of a project, its
justification.

c) Rationale   PRINCE2 offers a good set of
reports without unnecessary
progress meetings.

d) Rationale   Correct. PRINCE2 ensures that
all stakeholders are involved.
See the Communication
Management Strategy.

4. Which is NOT an aspect of   Correct Answer:
project performance to be
managed?

a) Costs   ☐
b) Timescales   ☐
c) Benefits   ☐
d) Delegation

Where to find the answer: 2.2

a) Rationale   Costs have to be managed,
hence the update of Stage and
Project Plans on a regular basis.

b) Rationale   Timescales have to be
managed, hence the update of
Stage and Project Plans on a
regular basis and the agreement
on target dates for Team Plans,
quality checks.

c) Rationale	The Business Case is reviewed at the end of each stage to ensure that the project is still viable and that the benefits are still achievable.
d) Rationale	Correct. Delegation is not one of the six areas of project performance to be managed.

5. Fill in the missing words in the following sentence.

Correct Answer:

The PRINCE2 processes address the [?] of the project.
□
a) shape and size □
b) chronological flow ☑
c) quality assurance □
d) formality □

Where to find the answer: 2.6

a) Rationale	No, the processes do not address the shape or size of a project. Any merging of processes or how many times a process needs to be used are considered as part of tailoring the method for a project.
b) Rationale	Correct. The processes address the flow from starting to closing a project.
c) Rationale	No, quality assurance sits outside a project. The Organization theme addresses how to involve quality assurance in a project.

d) Rationale

No, the formality will be mainly in how reports are made and the organization of the project management team. Processes look at what needs to be done and when.

6. Fill in the missing words in the following sentence.

Correct Answer:

PRINCE2 defines a project as a [?] that is created for the purpose of delivering business products.

☐

a) specialist stage   ☐
b) temporary structure   ☑
c) fixed set of resources   ☐
d) set of mandatory   ☐
   techniques

Where to find the answer: 1.1

a) Rationale

No, e.g. initiation is a stage in every PRINCE2 project, but is not a specialist stage.

b) Rationale

Correct. A project's team is assembled just for that project and is disbanded at the project close.

c) Rationale

No, the resources required may vary from stage to stage.

d) Rationale

No, PRINCE2 techniques are not mandatory. A company may already have, e.g., a quality checking technique, which it wishes to use in preference to the PRINCE2 quality review.

7. Which of the following are   Correct Answer:
    PRINCE2 plans?

    1. Exception Plan   ☐
    2. Stage Plan   ☐
    3. Quality Plan   ☐
    4. Benefits Review Plan   ☐
        a) 1, 2, 3   ☐
        b) 1, 2, 4   ☑
        c) 1, 3, 4   ☐
        d) 2, 3, 4   ☐

    Where to find the answer: 6.3.1

    a) Rationale   (4) There is a Benefits Review
                              Plan that describes how benefit
                              achievement will be checked.

    b) Rationale   Correct. (3) Although PRINCE2
                              discusses quality planning,
                              there is no separate Quality
                              Plan. Quality planning consists
                              of understanding the customer's
                              quality expectations and
                              acceptance criteria, creating a
                              Project Product Description, a
                              Quality Management Strategy
                              and a Quality Register.

    c) Rationale   (2) Every PRINCE2 stage has a
                              plan.

    d) Rationale   (1) An Exception Plan replaces
                              a plan that is forecast to deviate
                              outside its tolerances.

8. Which of the following are   Correct Answer:
    risk responses?

    1. Avoid   ☐
    2. Enhance   ☐

3. Fallback ☐
4. Ignore ☐
    a) 1, 2, 3 ☑
    b) 1, 2, 4 ☐
    c) 1, 3, 4 ☐
    d) 2, 3, 4 ☐

Where to find the answer:	Table 15.1
a) Rationale	Correct. (4) Risks are never ignored.
b) Rationale	(3) Fallback is a response prepared in case a known risk does occur. The risk may have been considered unlikely to occur, or too expensive to avoid or reduce.
c) Rationale	(2) A risk may be a threat or an opportunity. It may be sensible to enhance the chance of an opportunity occurring.
d) Rationale	(1) Risk avoidance is a sensible response.

9. Before the Risk Register is created where will the Project Manager record any risks?

    Correct Answer:

    a) Quality Register ☐
    b) Daily Log ☑
    c) Issue Register ☐
    d) Lessons Log ☐

Where to find the answer:	15.2.2
a) Rationale	The Quality Register records all planned quality checks, attendees and results.

b) Rationale

Correct. Risks are recorded here during *Starting up a Project* until the Risk Register is created during initiation.

c) Rationale

On analysis some issues may be recognized as risks, but if originally recognized as a risk, they would not be entered here.

d) Rationale

Lessons may come from how risks were dealt with, but new risks are not added to the Lessons Log.

10. What is the trigger for a project?

Correct Answer:

a) Project Initiation Documentation ☐

b) Project Brief ☐

c) Business Case ☐

d) Project Mandate ☑

Where to find the answer: 3

a) Rationale

The Project Initiation Documentation is not created until initiation and contains all the information required by the Project Board for it to decide if a project should be authorized.

b) Rationale

The Project Brief is used by the Project Board to decide if a project should be initiated and is based on the project mandate.

c) Rationale

The Business Case is not started until during the "Starting up a Project" process.

d) Rationale

Correct. The project mandate is provided by the responsible authority that is commissioning the project, and is the basis for the Project Brief.

11. In which process is the request for project funding defined in detail?

Correct Answer:

a) Starting up a Project ☐
b) Initiating a Project ☑
c) Directing a Project ☐
d) Closing a Project ☐

Where to find the answer: 4.7

a) Rationale

Only an outline Business Case is completed during *Starting up a Project*.

b) Rationale

Correct. The Project Plan and full Business Case are created here.

c) Rationale

Directing a Project covers the decision-making activities of the Project Board. Information such as the request for funding has to be prepared in other processes for presentation to the Project Board.

d) Rationale

A request for project funding has to be created before major resources are committed by the Project Board. When closing a project, there is a review to see whether the money was well-spent.

12. Which activities are carried
    out by the role of the quality
    review chair?

    Correct Answer:

    1. Check that the product is
       ready for review.   ☐
    2. Gather all question
       lists and set the review
       meeting agenda.   ☐
    3. Lead the review team
       through the product
       section by section.   ☐
    4. Ensure that all agreed
       errors are recorded on a
       follow-up action list.   ☐
       a) 1, 2, 3   ☐
       b) 1, 2, 4   ☑
       c) 1, 3, 4   ☐
       d) 2, 3, 4   ☐

Where to find the answer: 14.8.3

a) Rationale   (4) The chair ensures that all
                         agreed actions are recorded.

b) Rationale   Correct. (3) The presenter leads
                         the reviewers through the
                         product.

c) Rationale   (2) The chair is responsible for
                         creating the agenda from the
                         question lists.

d) Rationale   (1) The chair is responsible
                         for checking that the product
                         is ready for review, even if
                         the task is delegated to the
                         administrator.

13. Which does NOT involve the Project Board?

Correct Answer:

a) Exception assessment   ☐
b) Highlight Reports   ☐
c) Work Package authorization   ☑
d) Project closure   ☐

Where to find the answer: 6.1

a) Rationale

The Project Board reviews an Exception Plan during an exception assessment.

b) Rationale

The Project Board receives Highlight Reports from the Project Manager.

c) Rationale

Correct. Work Packages are authorised by the Project Manager after discussion with a Team Manager.

d) Rationale

Project closure must be approved by the Project Board.

14. Identify the missing words in the following sentence.

Correct Answer:

Effective risk management is a prerequisite of the [?] Principle.   ☐

a) focus on products   ☐
b) continued business justification   ☑
c) manage by exception   ☐
d) manage by stages   ☐

Where to find the answer:	15.1
a) Rationale	The focus on products relates mainly to quality and planning.
b) Rationale	Correct. Without effective risk management there will be no confidence that the project will meet its objectives.
c) Rationale	Manage by exception relates mainly to the use of tolerances.
d) Rationale	Manage by stages relates to controls and planning.

15. How are Principles characterized? Correct Answer:

a) Are capable of tailoring ☐
b) Justify the project ☐
c) Apply to every project ☑
d) Their use is optional ☐

Where to find the answer:	2.3
a) Rationale	Processes and themes may be tailored, but not the Principles.
b) Rationale	A project is justified by its Business Case.
c) Rationale	Correct. PRINCE2 Principles are universal and can be applied to every project, no matter how small.
d) Rationale	Principles are not optional. They provide a framework of good practice.

16. Which is independent of the project management team? Correct Answer:

a) Team Manager ☐

b) Project Assurance   ☐
c) Project Support   ☐
d) Quality Assurance   ☑

Where to find the answer: 14.6

a) Rationale   The Team Manager is part of the project management team.

b) Rationale   Project Assurance is part of a Project Board member's work, which may be delegated.

c) Rationale   Project Support is a project role.

d) Rationale   Correct. Quality assurance is a company-wide function responsible for all standards.

17. Which product defines the authorities for handling requests for change?   Correct Answer:

a) Communication Management Strategy   ☐
b) Configuration Management Strategy   ☑
c) Quality Management Strategy   ☐
d) Risk Management Strategy   ☐

Where to find the answer: 16.1.3

a) Rationale   This defines the content, frequency and medium of all project communications.

b) Rationale   Correct. This defines configuration management and change control procedures.

c) Rationale

Whilst quality can be affected by poor handling of requests for change, the Quality Management Strategy does not describe how to handle them.

d) Rationale

This only contains procedures for handling risks.

18. Which are basic business options?

Correct Answer:

1. Do nothing
2. Do less
3. Do something
4. Do the minimum
    a) 1, 2, 3 ☐
    b) 1, 2, 4 ☐
    c) 1, 3, 4 ☑
    d) 2, 3, 4 ☐

Where to find the answer: 10.5

a) Rationale

(4) 'Do the minimum' may be a business option.

b) Rationale

(3) 'Do something' includes all the positive business options.

c) Rationale

Correct. 'Do less' is not a business option.

d) Rationale

'Do nothing' is always a business option that should be considered.

19. Which part of the Business Case balances costs against benefits over a period of time?

Correct Answer:

a) Expected benefits ☐
b) Business options ☐

c) Investment appraisal ☑

d) Expected disbenefits ☐

Where to find the answer: 10.5

a) Rationale

This looks only at the benefits and does not include how much it will cost to obtain them.

b) Rationale

This lists the considered options on how to solve the business problem.

c) Rationale

Correct. This compares the project and maintenance costs against the benefit and savings value.

d) Rationale

This looks at the negative side of what the impact of the chosen option will bring.

20. Which role is responsible for realizing post-project benefits?

Correct Answer:

a) Executive ☐

b) Senior User ☑

c) Senior Supplier ☐

d) Project Manager ☐

Where to find the answer: 10.6

a) Rationale

The Executive is responsible for the Benefits Review Plan during the project, but not for checking how well the benefits have been achieved. Corporate management will manage post-project benefit reviews and expect the Senior User(s) to provide the evidence of realisation.

b) Rationale   Correct. As the Senior User
                                will be closest to those using
                                the final product, this role is
                                charged with checking on the
                                achievement of the benefits.

c) Rationale   The Senior Supplier may be
                                responsible for the supplier's
                                Business Case, but not for the
                                project's (customer's) Business
                                Case.

d) Rationale   The Project Manager is
                                responsible for reviewing any
                                changes to the Business Case
                                during the project and advising
                                the Executive.

21. Which of the following   Correct Answer:
    statements is FALSE?

    a) A company's quality   ☑
       management system
       becomes part of PRINCE2.

    b) Customer's quality   ☐
       expectations should be
       discovered in the *Starting
       up a Project* process.

    c) PRINCE2 may form part   ☐
       of a company's quality
       management system.

    d) The use of Team Plans is   ☐
       optional.

    Where to find the answer: 14.3.1, 14.5.1 and 12.2.3

    a) Rationale   Correct. A company's quality
                                    management system should
                                    cover standards for all its work,
                                    not just those for project work.

b) Rationale   Customer's quality expectations
                                    are discovered as part of the
                                    activity of preparing the outline
                                    Business Case.

c) Rationale   PRINCE2 may form that
                                    part of a company's quality
                                    management system that covers
                                    project work.

d) Rationale   A project may not need Team
                                    Plans, but the Project and Stage
                                    Plans are mandatory.

22. Which is NOT one of the   Correct Answer:
    four tasks of the Product-
    based Planning technique?

    a) Identifying dependencies   ☐
    b) Producing a Product   ☐
       Breakdown Structure
    c) Creating a Product   ☑
       Checklist
    d) Writing Product   ☐
       Descriptions of each
       significant product

    Where to find the answer: 12.4

    a) Rationale   Dependencies are identified
                                    when creating a Product Flow
                                    Diagram, part of Product-based
                                    Planning.

    b) Rationale   A Product Breakdown Structure
                                    is a hierarchical structure. Its
                                    creation is a task of Product-
                                    based Planning.

c) Rationale   Correct. Product checklists are an optional, tabular presentation of a plan; part of planning, but not of Product-based Planning.

d) Rationale   Writing Product Descriptions is an integral part of Product-based Planning.

23. Which of the following reviews the benefits achieved by the project?   Correct Answer:

a) End Project Report   ☐
b) Lessons Report   ☐
c) Post-project benefits review   ☑
d) Quality review   ☐

Where to find the answer: 10.6

a) Rationale   The End Project Report will identify any benefits achieved during the project cycle, but not those benefits that will be gained after the project closes.

b) Rationale   The Lessons Report does not cover benefit achievement and does not extend beyond the project cycle.

c) Rationale   Correct. The Benefits Review Plan sets out when and how the achievement of benefits is to be checked. The check is done in one or more post-project benefits reviews.

d) Rationale

A quality review only looks at the quality of a single product. There may be a quality review of the Benefits Review Plan, but it does not review benefit achievement.

24. Who is responsible for assessing and updating the Business Case at the end of a stage?

Correct Answer:

a) Senior User ☐
b) Executive ☐
c) Project Manager ☑
d) Project Assurance ☐

Where to find the answer: 8.3

a) Rationale

The Senior User, as a member of the Project Board, will review the updated Business Case as part of the decision on whether to authorize the next stage, but does not update it.

b) Rationale

The Executive is responsible for the Business Case during the project, but does not update it, only reviews it when presented by the Project Manager.

c) Rationale

Correct. The Project Manager does this as part of *Managing a Stage Boundary* for presentation to the Project Board.

d) Rationale

Project Assurance will verify any Business Case update by the Project Manager before its presentation to the Project Board.

25. Whose role is it to ensure that planned communications actually occur?

Correct Answer:

a) Project Board ☐
b) Project Manager ☐
c) Project Assurance ☑
d) Corporate management ☐

Where to find the answer: 11.9

a) Rationale

The Project Board has input into its own communication needs and those of stakeholders, but checking that these are met is part of Project Assurance.

b) Rationale

The Project Manager is responsible for creating most of the communications, but not for ensuring that they occur.

c) Rationale

Correct. Part of the Project Assurance role is to verify that what is planned in the Communication Management Strategy actually occurs.

d) Rationale

Corporate management will have an input of their communication needs, but monitoring that they receive communications is part of Project Assurance.

26. In which process is the Quality Management Strategy (QMS) created?

Correct Answer:

a) Starting up a Project	☐
b) Initiating a Project	☑
c) Directing a Project	☐
d) Managing a Stage Boundary	☐

Where to find the answer: 4.1

a) Rationale — No, the customer's quality expectations and acceptance criteria are established here, but they feed into initiation.

b) Rationale — Correct. As part of the Project Initiation Documentation, the Quality Management Strategy is created.

c) Rationale — No, *Directing a Project* does not cover the creation of any of the strategies, but covers the review of the Project Initiation Document in which they are held.

d) Rationale — No, the QMS is required to be in place before any stages are complete.

27. Which theme is central to the approach to quality?

Correct Answer:

a) Manage by exception	☐
b) Continued business justification	☐
c) Focus on products	☑
d) Defined roles and responsibilities	☐

Where to find the answer: 14.1

a) Rationale   No, an exception may be triggered by a threat to exceed quality tolerances, but this is only one of several reasons for an exception.

b) Rationale   No, this focuses on business justification for the project.

c) Rationale   Correct. Quality in PRINCE2 focuses on defining the quality of products in such things as writing Product Descriptions.

d) Rationale   No, roles will have some quality responsibilities, but this theme covers all project responsibilities, not just quality.

28. Which product relates planned quality activities to those actually performed?   Correct Answer:

a) Quality Register   ☑
b) Project approach   ☐
c) Quality Management Strategy   ☐
d) Lessons Log   ☐

Where to find the answer: 14.6

a) Rationale   Correct. The Quality Register contains an entry for every planned quality action, and is updated with the results of the inspection.

b) Rationale   No, the project approach describes how the provision of the selected business option will be done, and does not contain quality activities.

c) Rationale

No, the QMS defines the standards to be used and quality responsibilities, but not the detailed quality actions, which are not planned until planning each stage.

d) Rationale

No, the Lessons Log contains details of good or bad lessons found, and is not a record of planned quality actions.

29. Which action is NOT part of Accept a Work Package?

Correct Answer:

a) Agree upon tolerance margins. ☐
b) Understand the reporting requirements. ☐
c) Produce a Team Plan. ☐
d) Monitor and control any Work Package risks. ☑

Where to find the answer: 7.1

a) Rationale

This is part of the Team Manager's job when accepting a Work Package.

b) Rationale

This is part of the Team Manager's job when accepting a Work Package.

c) Rationale

This is part of the Team Manager's job before accepting a Work Package.

d) Rationale

Correct. Monitoring and control comes during the execution of a Work Package, after accepting it.

30. Comparing a product against   Correct Answer:
    defined criteria is an objective
    of what?

    a) Work Package   ☐
    b) Investment appraisal   ☐
    c) Quality review   ☑
    d) Quality Register   ☐

    Where to find the answer: 14.9.3

    a) Rationale   No, a Work Package is an
                                    agreement between the
                                    Project Manager and the Team
                                    Manager, but the Product
                                    Description contains the
                                    quality method and criteria.

    b) Rationale   No, this compares the cost of
                                    developing and maintaining
                                    a product against its expected
                                    benefit and savings value.

    c) Rationale   Correct. In a quality review, the
                                    reviewers compare a product
                                    against the quality criteria held
                                    in the Product Description.

    d) Rationale   No, the Quality Register
                                    contains a summary of the
                                    result of such a check.

31. Which process defines   Correct Answer:
    Quality responsibilities?

    a) Starting up a Project   ☐
    b) Initiating a Project   ☑
    c) Directing a Project   ☐
    d) Managing a Stage   ☐
       Boundary

Where to find the answer:	4.1
a) Rationale	No, customer's quality expectations are discovered here, but quality responsibilities are defined during initiation.
b) Rationale	Correct. The Quality Management Strategy is created during initiation.
c) Rationale	No, *Directing a Project* covers approval of the QMS as part of the Project Initiation Document, but not its creation.
d) Rationale	No, quality responsibilities have to be known before any specialist stages are undertaken.

32. Whose responsibility is it to check that a product is ready for its quality review?

Correct Answer:

a) Chair ☑
b) Administrator ☐
c) Presenter ☐
d) Reviewer ☐

Where to find the answer:	14.8.3
a) Rationale	Correct. Part of the role of quality review chair is to check that a product is ready when planned.
b) Rationale	No, the administrator may be delegated to do this by the chair, but it remains the chair's responsibility.

c) Rationale | No, the presenter is normally the person who has developed the product and therefore would not need to check whether it is ready for review.

d) Rationale | No, there may be a number of reviewers whose job is to look at the draft product. They do not carry out the check to see if the product is ready.

33. Whose task is it to produce products consistent with their Product Descriptions?

Correct Answer:

a) Senior User — ☐
b) Project Manager — ☐
c) Team Manager — ☑
d) Senior Supplier — ☐

Where to find the answer: 11.8

a) Rationale | No, the Senior User should approve the Product Descriptions.

b) Rationale | No, the Project Manager has responsibility for all project work, but delegates the production of products to the Team Managers.

c) Rationale | Correct. Products are created during the *Managing Product Delivery* process, which covers the Team Manager's work.

d) Rationale

No, the Senior Supplier is responsible for providing supplier resources and is accountable for the quality of all products delivered by supplier resources, but not at the detailed level of the actual production of them.

34. What provides the Business Case with planned costs?

Correct Answer:

a) Project Brief ☐
b) Project Plan ☑
c) Initiation Stage Plan ☐
d) Project Approach ☐

Where to find the answer: 12.2.1

a) Rationale

No, the Project Brief may not contain any costs. If it does, these are likely to be from an earlier feasibility study and too old or too vague to be used in the Business Case.

b) Rationale

Correct. The Project Plan contains the overall timeframe and the total cost of the project, which is why it must precede refinement of the Business Case.

c) Rationale

No, the initiation Stage Plan only contains the cost of initiation.

d) Rationale

No, the project approach does not contain costs, just a description of the way in which the selected business option will be provided.

35. What is identified first in the PRINCE2 planning philosophy?

Correct Answer:

a) Dependencies ☐
b) Activities ☐
c) Products ☑
d) Resources ☐

Where to find the answer: 12.3

a) Rationale

No, dependencies cannot be identified until there are products or activities that may have dependencies between them.

b) Rationale

In PRINCE2, activities are based on the products they are to produce or obtain.

c) Rationale

Correct. PRINCE2 planning is product-based. After identifying the required products, their dependencies and then the activities required to produce the products are identified.

d) Rationale

No, resources are not considered until the products, their activities, dependencies and effort required are known.

36. In which process is the means of reviewing benefits developed?

Correct Answer:

a) Closing a Project ☐
b) Initiating a Project ☑
c) Managing a Stage Boundary ☐
d) Starting up a Project ☐

Where to find the answer: 4.7

a) Rationale — No, the Benefits Review Plan is reviewed and possibly updated here, but it is created at the beginning of the project.

b) Rationale — Correct. The Benefits Review Plan is created during initiation.

c) Rationale — No, the means of reviewing benefits may be reviewed here for any changes, but it is created during initiation.

d) Rationale — No, work on this will not be done until the Project Board has authorized initiation.

37. In which process are previous lessons captured?

Correct Answer:

a) Starting up a Project ☑
b) Initiating a Project ☐
c) Managing a Stage Boundary ☐
d) Closing a Project ☐

Where to find the answer:	3.2
a) Rationale	Correct. The Lessons Reports of earlier projects are reviewed here and any that may apply to the current project copied to the Lessons Log.
b) Rationale	No, when creating all initiation products the Lessons Log is checked for any earlier lessons that may apply to them.
c) Rationale	No, there may be lessons from the current project that make it worthwhile to create a Lessons Report during this process, but lessons from earlier projects will have been captured during start-up.
d) Rationale	No, lessons from the current project are written up in a Lessons Report for future projects.

38. Which product defines whether the solution will be developed in-house?

Correct Answer:

a) Project mandate ☐
b) Project approach ☑
c) Business Case ☐
d) Project Plan ☐

Where to find the answer:	3.5
a) Rationale	If the project is part of a programme, there may be information in the project mandate that makes it clear what the project approach has to be, but it is formally defined in the project approach.

b) Rationale	Correct. The purpose of the project approach is to identify the type of solution to the chosen business option, where an in-house development is one of the possibilities.
c) Rationale	No, the Business Case contains the selected option to resolve the business problem, such as falling sales, but does not say how that option is to be delivered.
d) Rationale	The Project Plan is based on the project approach.

39. Which process ensures that there is an interface with corporate management throughout the project?

Correct Answer:

a) Starting up a Project   ☐
b) Managing a Stage Boundary   ☐
c) Directing a Project   ☑
d) Initiating a Project   ☐

Where to find the answer: 4.4

a) Rationale	No, corporate management will perform some of the work of starting up, such as appointing the Executive, but the process only covers pre-project work.
b) Rationale	No, this will simply follow any requirements laid down in the Communication Management Strategy.

| c) Rationale | Correct. It is a responsibility of the Project Board to maintain communication links with corporate. How and when this is done will be described in the Communication Management Strategy. |
| d) Rationale | The Communication Management Strategy is created here, but the initiation process does not run throughout the project. |

40. Which statement is NOT a purpose of the *Closing a Project* process?

Correct Answer:

a) Confirm acceptance by the customer of the project's products. ☐

b) Recognize that the project has nothing more to contribute. ☐

c) Recognize that approved changes to the objectives in the Project Initiation Document have been achieved. ☐

d) Place formal requirements on accepting and delivering project work. ☑

Where to find the answer: 9

a) Rationale   Acceptance of the project's products is formally done as part of closing a project.

b) Rationale

Whether the project is being closed normally or prematurely, the *Closing a Project* process has to confirm to the Project Board that the project has nothing more to contribute and should therefore be closed.

c) Rationale

A major part of *Closing a Project* is to compare how the project performed in meeting the Project Initiation Document. Any changes made to the Project Initiation Document during the project must be included to make this comparison meaningful.

d) Rationale

Correct. This is far too late to define acceptance of project work. This must be done before delivery of any specialist products occurs.

41. Which is NOT a Project Board activity?

Correct Answer:

a) Authorize initiation ☐
b) Give ad hoc direction ☐
c) Authorize a Work Package ☑
d) Authorize the project ☐

Where to find the answer: 6.1

a) Rationale

This is the first decision made by the Project Board after *Starting up a Project*.

b) Rationale | This is an ongoing Project Board activity, reviewing Highlight Reports, any Exception Reports and passing external information to the Project Manager.

c) Rationale | Correct. This is a Project Manager activity.

d) Rationale | This is the second decision of the Project Board after initiation.

42. What information is the trigger for the *Starting up a Project* process?

Correct Answer:

a) Project mandate ☑
b) Project Initiation Document ☐
c) An appointed Executive ☐
d) Outline Business Case ☐

Where to find the answer: 3

a) Rationale | Correct. The project mandate is the trigger for this process.

b) Rationale | No, the Project Initiation Document is not created until the initiation stage.

c) Rationale | No, the Executive is appointed during *Starting up a Project*.

d) Rationale | No, the outline Business Case is created during *Starting up a Project*.

43. Which of the following is   Correct Answer:
    NOT input to the Project
    Board?

    a) Informal request for   ☐
       advice
    b) Escalated Issue Report   ☐
    c) Project authorization   ☑
       notification
    d) Highlight Report   ☐

    Where to find the answer: 5.2.3

    a) Rationale   Informal requests for advice
                                      from the Project Board can be
                                      made at any time by the Project
                                      Manager.

    b) Rationale   This can be input to the Project
                                      Board for an opinion before
                                      the Project Manager raises an
                                      Exception Report.

    c) Rationale   Correct. This is sent by the
                                      Project Board to corporate
                                      management as part of
                                      authorising the project to tell
                                      them that the project has been
                                      started.

    d) Rationale   This is sent to the Project Board
                                      by the Project Manager on a
                                      regular frequency.

44. Which document contains   Correct Answer:
    any follow-on action
    recommendations?

    a) Lessons Report
    b) End Stage Report   ☐

c) End Project Report   ☑
d) Benefits Review Plan   ☐

Where to find the answer: 9.4.3

a) Rationale   No, this forms a part of the
                                   End Project Report together
                                   with the follow-on action
                                   recommendations.

b) Rationale   No, follow-on action
                                   recommendations are only
                                   assembled at project closure
                                   time.

c) Rationale   Correct. Follow-on action
                                   recommendations form part of
                                   the End Project Report, and are
                                   then separated and sent on to
                                   the team that will maintain the
                                   product.

d) Rationale   No, this is only a plan of when
                                   and how to measure benefit
                                   realisation.

45. Which product captures user   Correct Answer:
    quality expectations and
    acceptance criteria?

a) Project Product   ☑
   Description
b) Quality Management   ☐
   Strategy
c) Project Brief   ☐
d) Daily Log   ☐

Where to find the answer: 3.4.3

a) Rationale

Correct. This documents the expectations and describes the standards and processes that will be needed in order to achieve that quality.

b) Rationale

No, this describes the standards and techniques that will be used, that is it follows on from the Project Product Description's statement of quality needs and says what the project has found to match those quality checking needs.

c) Rationale

No, this describes what the project needs to achieve, objectives, scope and constraints, but not the quality expectations.

d) Rationale

This is a diary of recorded events, actions, notes for the Project Manager or Team Manager.

46. Which of the following are done in the *Starting up a Project* process?   Correct Answer:

1. Set up the project management team.
2. Develop the project mandate into the Project Brief.

3. Create the Issue Register.   ☐
4. Devise the project   ☐
   approach.
     a) 1, 2, 3   ☐
     b) 1, 2, 4   ☑
     c) 1, 3, 4   ☐
     d) 2, 3, 4   ☐

Where to find the answer: 3 and 4.3.4

   a) Rationale   (4) The project approach is
                         devised during *Starting up a
                         Project*.

   b) Rationale   Correct. (3) The Issue Register is
                         not created until the initiation
                         process.

   c) Rationale   (2) The project mandate is
                         enhanced to become the
                         Project Brief during the *Starting
                         up a Project* process.

   d) Rationale   (1) The project management
                         team is devised and appointed
                         during *Starting up a Project*.

47. An example of Work Package   Correct Answer:
    [?] might be 'I need this by
    Thursday close of work, but
    by Friday lunchtime at the
    latest'.

   a) Approval requirements   ☐
   b) Constraints   ☐
   c) Tolerance   ☑
   d) Reporting and problem   ☐
      handling

Where to find the answer:	6.1.3
a) Rationale	No, approval requirements say who has to approve the completed products of the Work Package and how.
b) Rationale	No, these are constraints on the work, such as people to be involved, rules to be followed.
c) Rationale	Correct. Tolerance gives a range, in this case of time, within which the delivery is acceptable.
d) Rationale	No, this covers any need for Checkpoint Reports or what the Team Manager has to do if a problem occurs, e.g. raise an issue to the Project Manager.

48. Configuration management is described in which theme?

Correct Answer:

a) Quality ☐
b) Plans ☐
c) Progress ☐
d) Change ☑

Where to find the answer:	16.1
a) Rationale	No, quality will suffer without configuration management, but it is not described here.
b) Rationale	No, plans need to be configuration managed, but how this is to be done is not described here.
c) Rationale	No, progress covers tolerances, monitoring and reporting.

d) Rationale

Correct. This theme covers
configuration management and
change control.

49. Which are purposes of a
summary risk profile?

Correct Answer:

1. Shows the risk owners   ☐
2. Snapshot of the risk   ☐
environment
3. Shows risk trends   ☐
4. Identifies risks beyond the   ☐
risk appetite
  a) 1, 2, 3   ☐
  b) 1, 2, 4   ☐
  c) 1, 3, 4   ☐
  d) 2, 3, 4   ☑

Where to find the answer: 15.3.2.1

a) Rationale

(4) The risk tolerance line can
be drawn on the profile to
identify risks that would be
beyond it.

b) Rationale

(3) A combination of several
snapshots of the risk profile
over a period of time would
reveal any risk trends.

c) Rationale

(2) A summary risk profile is a
snapshot of risk probability and
impact at one moment in time.

d) Rationale

Correct. (1) A summary risk
profile does not show risk
owners.

50. In which process is the   Correct Answer:
    Business Case reviewed and
    updated?

    a) Controlling a Stage   ☐
    b) Managing Product   ☐
       Delivery
    c) Managing a Stage   ☑
       Boundary
    d) Directing a Project   ☐

    Where to find the answer: 8.3

    a) Rationale   *Controlling a Stage* checks the
                                  Business Case for impact of
                                  new risks or issues, but does
                                  not update it.

    b) Rationale   The *Managing Product Delivery*
                                  process has nothing to do with
                                  the Business Case.

    c) Rationale   Correct. The Business Case is
                                  updated against the Project
                                  Plan with actuals from the
                                  current stage and the next
                                  Stage Plan, plus any issues or
                                  risks that may affect it.

    d) Rationale   *Directing a Project* will be
                                  shown the updated Business
                                  Case, but does not cover its
                                  updating.

51. Which is NOT part of an   Correct Answer:
    unambiguous identification
    of a risk?

    a) Probability   ☑
    b) Cause   ☐

c) Effect   ☐
d) Event   ☐

Where to find the answer: 15.3.1.1

a) Rationale   Correct. Probability is part of
                                    the analysis of a risk, once it
                                    has been identified.

b) Rationale   Cause is part of a risk
                                    statement, e.g. 'Because of the
                                    heavy rain …'.

c) Rationale   Effect is the impact of the risk,
                                    e.g. 'leading to closure of the
                                    golf course'.

d) Rationale   Event is the actual risk, e.g. 'the
                                    greens may be under water'.

52. What does the triggering of   Correct Answer:
    an early warning indicator
    provide?

a) Proximity of a risk.   ☐
b) A project objective could   ☑
   be at risk.
c) A note to the Project   ☐
   Board advising it of a
   forthcoming deviation
   beyond tolerance.
d) Date of a stage end   ☐
   approaching.

Where to find the answer: 15.2.5

a) Rationale   Proximity is an assessment of
                                    how soon a risk might occur –
                                    not an early warning.

b) Rationale	Correct. An early warning indicator is a piece of information that is monitored because it may reveal that one or more of the project's objectives could be at risk. For example, if you are worried that you might catch a cold, your temperature would be an early warning indicator.
c) Rationale	No, it is concerned with risks, not tolerances.
d) Rationale	Early warning indicators are like barometers, and are not dates.

53. What does a risk budget cover?   Correct Answer:

a) Cost of risks carried over to follow-on action recommendations	☐
b) Off-specification costs	☐
c) Costs of administering risk management	☐
d) Cost of fallback plans	☑

Where to find the answer: 15.3

a) Rationale	No, a risk budget is for use within a project, not post-project.
b) Rationale	No, an off-specification is not a risk. It is a known failure to meet some part of the specification or plan.

c) Rationale

No, the cost of risk administration should be built into a plan, whereas a risk budget is only spent if a fallback plan has to be used.

d) Rationale

Correct. Fallback plans are prepared in case a known risk occurs, and they require a risk budget.

54. Which document contains the Change Control procedure?

Correct Answer:

a) Quality Management Strategy   ☐

b) Configuration Management Strategy   ☑

c) Risk Management Strategy   ☐

d) Communication Management Strategy   ☐

Where to find the answer: 16.1.3

a) Rationale

No, the QMS does not contain the change control or configuration management procedures.

b) Rationale

Correct. Configuration management is closely linked with change control and both are covered in the Configuration Management Strategy.

c) Rationale

Risk management has nothing to do with change control or configuration.

d) Rationale

The Communication Management Strategy defines who needs what information at what frequency and who should supply it. It does not cover change control.

55. What is product status accounting?

Correct Answer:

a) Recording Work Package progress from a review of timesheets and the Team Plan

☐

b) An audit comparing actual product status with that shown in the Configuration Item Records

☐

c) Reporting on the current and historical state of products

☑

d) A summary of the state of the Quality Register at the end of a stage

☐

Where to find the answer:

16.1.5

a) Rationale

This is done in the activity *Review the Work Package Status* and looks at information from the Team Manager, not from the configuration library.

b) Rationale

This is a configuration audit, not a Product Status Account.

c) Rationale

Correct. The Project Manager can call for a Product Status Account at any time to view the current state of products or their history.

d) Rationale

This would form part of the End Stage Report, not a Product Status Account.

56. What is the second step in an Issue and Change Control procedure?

Correct Answer:

a) Decide ☐
b) Capture ☐
c) Propose ☐
d) Examine ☑

Where to find the answer: 16.3

a) Rationale   This follows the proposal step.

b) Rationale   This is the first step.

c) Rationale   This step follows the examination.

d) Rationale   Correct. This is the second step following capture.

57. Which Principle is NOT supported by the Progress theme?

Correct Answer:

a) Manage by exception ☐
b) Continued business justification ☐
c) Tailoring PRINCE2 ☑
d) Manage by stages ☐

Where to find the answer:	13.1
a) Rationale	Management by exception forms a key part of the progress theme, being linked to the use of tolerances.
b) Rationale	Part of Progress is monitoring, and one of the things monitored is the Business Case at such progress points as end stage assessments.
c) Rationale	Correct. The Progress theme does not describe how controls can be modified for different implementations of the PRINCE2 method.
d) Rationale	The breakdown of a project into stages is a central part of Progress, where the Project Board reviews the continued business justification.

58. Who sets project tolerances?   Correct Answer:

a) Corporate management   ☑
b) Project Board   ☐
c) Project Manager   ☐
d) Executive   ☐

Where to find the answer:	13.2.5.3
a) Rationale	Correct. This should be part of a project mandate, but the Executive may have to find out what they are by questioning corporate management during *Starting up a Project*.

b) Rationale | No, the Project Board sets stage tolerances within the project tolerances given to them by corporate management.

c) Rationale | No, the Project Manager receives stage tolerances from the Project Board and sets Work Package tolerances for a Team Manager.

d) Rationale | No, the Executive has to find out from corporate management what the project tolerances are.

59. Why might dividing a project into a small number of lengthy stages be a problem?

Correct Answer:

a) Makes project planning more difficult ☐

b) Increases project management administration costs ☐

c) Reduces the level of Project Board control ☑

d) Reduces the amount of risk monitoring ☐

Where to find the answer: 13.2.4.1

a) Rationale | The Project Plan may show where the stage boundaries occur, but they do not affect the difficulty of preparing it.

b) Rationale   A smaller number of controls for the Project Board may mean problems are seen later than with more stage breaks, but having fewer stages does not automatically increase administration costs. In fact, fewer stage ends may mean lower administration costs.

c) Rationale   Correct. A major Project Board control is end stage assessment, so longer but fewer stages would mean fewer control points for it.

d) Rationale   Risks are monitored throughout the stages, not just at end stage assessment times.

60. Which is an event-driven control?   Correct Answer:

a) Highlight Report   ☐
b) Checkpoint Report   ☐
c) End Stage Report   ☑
d) Review Work Package status   ☐

Where to find the answer: 13.4

a) Rationale   Highlight Reports are produced at a regular frequency, so are time-driven.

b) Rationale   Checkpoint Reports are produced at a frequency defined in a Work Package, so are another time-driven control.

c) Rationale	Correct. The end of a stage triggers this.
d) Rationale	No actual frequency is laid down for this activity, but it is a regular review, normally done weekly, and is not triggered by a specific event.

61. Which product is NOT reviewed when reviewing Work Package status?

Correct Answer:

a) Checkpoint Report ☐
b) Project Plan ☑
c) Team Plan ☐
d) Quality Register ☐

Where to find the answer: 6.2.3

a) Rationale	This is reviewed.
b) Rationale	Correct. The activity looks at Checkpoint Reports, Team Plans, the registers and the Configuration Item Records for the products involved.
c) Rationale	This is reviewed.
d) Rationale	This is reviewed.

62. Where are suitable reviewers first identified for a quality review?

Correct Answer:

a) Quality Management Strategy ☐
b) Project Plan ☐
c) Quality review preparation step ☐
d) Stage Plan ☑

Where to find the answer: 8.1.3

a) Rationale — The Quality Management Strategy identifies standards, quality techniques and quality responsibilities at a high level, but not for individual quality checks.

b) Rationale — The Project Plan does not go down to the level of detail where individual quality checks are identified.

c) Rationale — The quality review preparation step is where reviewers are given the product to prepare their question lists.

d) Rationale — Correct. The Project Manager should identify at least the chair of each quality review and possibly some reviewers when planning a stage.

63. Which of the following statements are TRUE?

Correct Answer:

1. The Executive role is responsible for the business interests of the customer and supplier.
2. There will always be two Business Cases in customer/supplier situations.
3. The customer and supplier may be part of the same corporate body, or may be independent of each other.

4. A project's Business Case
   means the customer's
   Business Case.
   a) 1, 2, 3   ☐
   b) 1, 2, 4   ☐
   c) 1, 3, 4   ☐
   d) 2, 3, 4   ☑

Where to find the answer: 10.1 and 10.3

a) Rationale   (4) A project concentrates on
                        the customer's Business Case.

b) Rationale   (3) Supplier resources may
                        come from the customer's
                        company or be from third-party
                        suppliers.

c) Rationale   (2) The customer has a Business
                        Case to define if the project
                        will bring sufficient benefits to
                        warrant the costs. The supplier
                        has a Business Case to see if
                        the commitment of resources
                        will bring a profit.

d) Rationale   Correct. (1) The Executive
                        is only responsible for the
                        customer's Business Case.

64. Which product reviews a   Correct Answer:
   project's actual achievements
   against the Project Initiation
   Document?

   a) Lessons Report   ☐
   b) Follow-on action   ☐
      recommendations
   c) End Project Report   ☑
   d) Benefits Review Plan   ☐

Where to find the answer: 9.4.3

a) Rationale   The Lessons Report provides any useful information on what went well and what went badly in terms of such things as the project management method and the techniques used.

b) Rationale   Follow-on action recommendations are items that are still outstanding at the close of the project and need to be passed to those who will maintain the product.

c) Rationale   Correct. The End Project Report describes how well the project met the requirements of the Project Initiation Document, not how successful the final product is at achieving its expected benefits.

d) Rationale   The Benefits Review Plan describes when and how achievement of the expected benefits can be measured.

65. Which product records a forecast failure to meet a requirement?   Correct Answer:

a) Risk Register   ☐
b) Concession   ☐
c) Highlight Report   ☐
d) Off-specification   ☑

Where to find the answer:	16.2.4
a) Rationale	A risk is something that might happen. A forecast failure is something that will happen and needs action now.
b) Rationale	A concession is an acceptance by the Project Board of an off-specification.
c) Rationale	A Highlight Report is a regular progress report from the Project Manager to the Project Board.
d) Rationale	Correct. This records some failure or forecast failure to meet either part of the product's specification or part of the Project Initiation Document, such as the Project Plan.

66. What product would the Project Manager call for when reviewing stage status to check on a phased hand-over of products?

Correct Answer:

a) Stage Plan   ☐
b) Quality Register   ☐
c) Product Status Account   ☑
d) Risk Register   ☐

Where to find the answer:	6.4.3
a) Rationale	This would give a general indication that work on the products involved has completed, but more precise information is needed.

b) Rationale

The Quality Register would show that any checks on the products have been completed, but there may be other work to assemble the package that would not be shown here.

c) Rationale

Correct. A Product Status Account would confirm whether the relevant products have been tested and accepted.

d) Rationale

The Risk Register might show whether there is a risk open about a product that is to be part of the phased hand-over, but the fact that it is complete and has been accepted is more significant.

67. Who should prepare the outline Business Case?

Correct Answer:

a) Senior User ☐
b) Executive ☑
c) Project Manager ☐
d) Corporate Management ☐

Where to find the answer: 10.3

a) Rationale

The Senior User will be asked to contribute and will be responsible after the project to verify that the benefits were achieved, but the Senior User does not produce the outline.

b) Rationale	Correct. The Executive checks to see if information for the outline Business Case was included in the project mandate, otherwise has to produce it during *Starting up a Project*.
c) Rationale	The Project Manager may be consulted for advice on what is required, but is not responsible.
d) Rationale	Corporate management may have included the relevant information in the project mandate, but often does not.

68. If an issue can be dealt with informally, where should a note of it be made?

Correct Answer:

a) Issue Register   ☐
b) Daily Log   ☑
c) Lessons Log   ☐
d) Risk Register   ☐

Where to find the answer: 16.3.1

a) Rationale	Entry here means that the issue is being dealt with formally.
b) Rationale	Correct. This avoids the need for document completion and administrative work, whilst ensuring that a record is kept.
c) Rationale	This records after the event anything that might be useful in the future, but is not used to trigger any action to resolve that particular issue.

d) Rationale	An entry here would mean that the issue was not only being dealt with formally, but had been assessed to be a risk.

69. Which of these statements is FALSE?   Correct Answer:

a) The Project Board approves Team Plans.	☑
b) The Project Board approves a stage Exception Plan.	☐
c) A Stage Plan is required for each stage in the Project Plan.	☐
d) The Project Plan is an overview of the total project.	☐

Where to find the answer: 6.1.3

a) Rationale	Correct. The Project Manager approves Team Plans.
b) Rationale	Only the Project Board can approve a stage Exception Plan.
c) Rationale	You need a Stage Plan, however simple, for initiation. In small projects it may be possible to physically add the content of, say, the single specialist stage to the Project Plan, but they are still separate plans.
d) Rationale	The Project Plan should not have too much detail to prevent the Project Board seeing the major product deliveries and timings.

70. When would an Exception   Correct Answer:
    Report be required?

    a) Whenever a new risk is   ☐
       identified.
    b) When a stakeholder raises   ☐
       a complaint.
    c) When a request for   ☐
       change or off-specification
       is received.
    d) When a stage is forecast   ☑
       to deviate outside its
       tolerance bounds.

    Where to find the answer: 16.3.4

    a) Rationale   The Project Board should not
                                    be involved in every small
                                    detail. The risk may be unlikely
                                    to occur or a response can be
                                    found to take care of it without
                                    asking for a Project Board
                                    decision.

    b) Rationale   A complaint may be many
                                    things that are not connected
                                    with a deviation beyond
                                    tolerances and can be dealt
                                    with in other ways.

    c) Rationale   It is too early to know. Without
                                    analysis it is not known on
                                    receipt of an issue whether
                                    it will cause an exception
                                    situation.

    d) Rationale   Correct. The Project Board must
                                    be informed and an Exception
                                    Report defines the information
                                    it needs.

71. What is the final step in risk management?

Correct Answer:

a) Appoint a risk owner ☐
b) Decide ☐
c) Communicate ☑
d) Implement ☐

Where to find the answer: 15.3

a) Rationale — This is part of the implementation.

b) Rationale — Decision has to be followed by implementation.

c) Rationale — Correct. Having reviewed the risk and decided what action to take, it is necessary to inform the relevant people.

d) Rationale — You implement the decision and then communicate what has been done.

72. When tailoring PRINCE2 for a project, which Principles can be omitted?

Correct Answer:

a) None ☑
b) All except continued business justification ☐
c) Manage by stages ☐
d) Manage by exception ☐

Where to find the answer: 17.3.1

a) Rationale — Correct. The Principles are universal in that they apply to every project.

b) Rationale — Every project should be justified.

| c) Rationale | Every PRINCE2 project has at least two stages, the first being initiation, however short. |
| d) Rationale | Any project should have tolerances set, and therefore the Principle of manage by exception is always required. |

73. In tailoring a project within a programme environment, why might responsibility for the Benefits Review Plan be removed from the Executive's role?

Correct Answer:

a) It might be given to the Senior User ☐

b) There may be no project benefits to be reviewed ☐

c) It could be moved to Project Assurance ☐

d) It becomes a programme responsibility ☑

Where to find the answer: 10.3

| a) Rationale | The Senior User is responsible for the work of checking benefit achievement, but the Executive is responsible for the plan. |
| b) Rationale | Without offering any benefits the project should not have started. |

c) Rationale	Project Assurance only monitors on behalf of the Project Board, but does not have responsibility for producing any product other than, possibly, a configuration audit.
d) Rationale	Correct. The project may simply be contributing to the programme's benefits and may not have its own Benefits Review Plan.

74. Which project role would sit on the programme board?

Correct Answer:

a) None ☐
b) Senior Supplier ☐
c) Executive ☑
d) Quality assurance ☐

Where to find the answer: 17.3.2

a) Rationale	Communication and decisions at programme level affect the projects and should have representation.
b) Rationale	The Senior Supplier for one project may not be involved in other projects in the programme and is not defined as having a possible programme board role.
c) Rationale	Correct. The Executives of the various projects of a programme would sit on the programme board to ensure they all contribute to the same objectives and strategy.

| d) Rationale | Quality assurance has a company-wide role, but is not a programme or project decision-maker. |

75. Which theme is most affected when used in simple projects?

Correct Answer:

a) Business Case	☐
b) Organisation	☑
c) Risk	☐
d) Change	☐

Where to find the answer: 17.3.2

a) Rationale	The Business Case may be simpler, but will not be greatly affected.
b) Rationale	Correct. Several roles may be combined in simple projects.
c) Rationale	Risk will still be present in simple projects.
d) Rationale	Even the simplest of projects may be subject to change. Failure to control changes will result in loss of control of the project.